SO-AEW-490

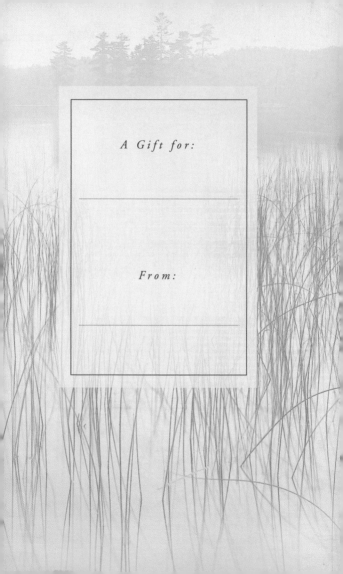

A Gift for:

_____

From:

_____

GOD'S
MESSAGE
FOR EACH DAY

*Wisdom
from
the Word
of God*

EUGENE H.
PETERSON

BOK5109

Copyright © 2004 by Eugene H. Peterson.

Published under license from J. Countryman®, a trademark of
Thomas Nelson, Inc., exclusively for Hallmark Cards, Inc.

Published in association with the literary agency of Alive
Communications, Inc., 1465 Kelly Johnson Blvd., Suite 320,
Colorado Springs, CO 80920.

Compiled and edited by Terri Gibbs.

All rights reserved. No portion of this publication may be repro-
duced, stored in a retrieval system or transmitted in any form by any
means—electronic, mechanical, photocopying, recording, or any
other—except for brief quotations in printed reviews, without the
prior written permission of the publisher.

Scripture quotations in this book are from the following sources:

The Message (THE MESSAGE) © 1993. Used by permission of
NavPress Publishing Group.

The New King James Version (NKJV) ©1979, 1980, 1982, 1992,
Thomas Nelson, Inc., Publisher.

The Revised Standard Version of the Bible (RSV) © 1946, 1952,
1971, 1973 by the Division of Christian Education of the National
Council of the Churches of Christ in the USA. Used by permission.

The New Revised Standard Version Bible (NRSV). Copyright © 1989 by
the Division of Christian Education of the National Council of the
Churches of Christ in the United States of America. Used by permission.

Designed by UDG|DesignWorks, Sisters, Oregon.

ISBN: 1-4041-0179-9

Visit us on the Web at www.Hallmark.com.
www.thomasnelson.com
www.jcountryman.com

Printed and bound in China.

Nothing counts more
in the way we live
than what
we believe about God.

*God is the living center
of everything.*

GOD IS SURE OF US

God will never let you down;
he'll never let you be pushed past your limit.

1 CORINTHIANS 10:13, THE MESSAGE

We wander like lost sheep, true; but God is a faithful shepherd who pursues us relentlessly. We have our ups and downs, zealously believing one day and gloomily doubting the next, but He is faithful. We break our promises, but He doesn't break His. Discipleship is not a contract in which if we break our part of the agreement He is free to break His; it is a covenant in which He established the conditions and guarantees the results. . . .

All the persons of faith I know are sinners, doubters, uneven performers. We are secure not because we are sure of ourselves but because we trust that God is sure of us.

A LONG OBEDIENCE

GOD LISTENS

Open up before God, keep nothing back;
he'll do whatever needs to be done.

PSALM 37:5, THE MESSAGE

We live in a noisy world. We are yelled at, promoted, called. Everyone has an urgent message for us. We are surrounded with noise: telephone, radio, television, stereo. Messages are amplified deafeningly. The world is a mob in which everyone is talking at once and no one is willing or able to listen. But God listens. He not only speaks to us, he listens to us. His listening to us is an even greater marvel than his speaking to us. It is rare to find anyone who listens carefully and thoroughly. . . .

When it happens we know that what we say and feel are immensely important. We acquire dignity. We never know how well we think or speak until we find someone who listens.

REVERSED THUNDER

PIECES OF LIFE

"Then give Caesar what is his,
and give God what is his."

MATTHEW 22:21, THE MESSAGE

"Our citizenship is in heaven," say those who pray, and they are ardent in pursuing the prizes of that place. But this passion for the unseen in no way detracts from their involvement in daily affairs: working well and playing fair, signing petitions and paying taxes, rebuking the wicked and encouraging the righteous, getting wet in the rain and smelling the flowers. Theirs is a tremendous, kaleidoscopic assemblage of bits and pieces of touched, smelled, seen and tasted reality that is received and offered in acts of prayer.

WHERE YOUR TREASURE IS

LIVING WELL

*Help me understand these things inside and
out so I can ponder your miracle-wonders.*

PSALM 119:27, THE MESSAGE

What do Bible stories tell us about living
this human life well, living it totally?
Primarily and mostly they tell us that it means
dealing with God. It means dealing with a lot
of other things as well: danger and parents and
enemies and friends and lovers and children and
wives and pride and humiliation and . . . sickness
and death and sexuality . . . and fear and peace—
to say nothing of diapers . . . and breakfast and
traffic jams and clogged drainpipes and bounced
checks. But always, at the forefront and in the
background of circumstances, events, and people,
it's God.

LEAP OVER A WALL

WE ARE BECOMING

When the Complete arrives,
our incompletes will be canceled.

1 CORINTHIANS 13:10, THE MESSAGE

N ot one of us, at this moment, is complete. In another hour, another day, we will have changed. We are in process of becoming either less or more. There are a million chemical and electrical interchanges going on in each of us this very moment. There are intricate moral decisions and spiritual transactions taking place. What are we becoming? Less or more?

RUN WITH THE HORSES

PEOPLE IN COMMUNITY

How wonderful, how beautiful,
when brothers and sisters get along!

PSALM 133:1, THE MESSAGE

The psalm puts into song what is said and demonstrated throughout Scripture and church: community is essential. Scripture knows nothing of the solitary Christian. People of faith are always members of a community. Creation itself was not complete until there was community, Adam needing Eve before humanity was whole. God never works with individuals in isolation, but always with people in community.

A LONG OBEDIENCE

DIRECTION AND PURPOSE

Live freely, animated and motivated by God's Spirit.
Then you won't feed the compulsions of selfishness.

GALATIANS 5:16, THE MESSAGE

In the Christian way we acquire a healthy value system. We find that persons are more important than property. We learn that forgiveness is preferable to property. We learn that forgiveness is preferable to revenge. We realize that worshiping God is more central than impressing our neighbors.

Without values we live "in vain." If we lose touch with our values, we are at the mercy of every seduction, every inducement, every claim on our money, our energy, our time. Values infuse life with a steady sense of direction and purpose.

TRAVELING LIGHT

GOD DOESN'T GET BORED

Absolutely nothing can get between us and God's love.

ROMANS 8:39, THE MESSAGE

The only serious mistake we can make when illness comes, when anxiety threatens, when conflict disturbs our relationships with others is to conclude that God has gotten bored looking after us and has shifted his attention to a more exciting Christian. Or that God has become disgusted with our meandering obedience and decided to let us fend for ourselves for a while. Or that God has gotten too busy fulfilling prophecy in the Middle East to take time now to sort out the complicated mess we have gotten ourselves into. That is the *only* serious mistake we can make.

A Long Obedience

THE LORD IS MIGHTY

Mightier than the thunders of many waters,
mightier than the waves
of the sea, the LORD on high is mighty!

PSALM 93:4, RSV

If God is not sovereign, I do, in fact, live in chaos. Randomness and chance permeate the universe. On the other hand, if God rules, there is foundational order. No accident is sheer accident. No chaos is ultimate. . . . Whatever other wills, powers, and influences I live under and among, one is first and last, foundational and final: "The LORD on high is mighty!"

WHERE YOUR TREASURE IS

GOD'S GREAT GIFT

GOD is magnificent; he can never be praised enough.

PSALM 145:3, THE MESSAGE

W e believe that this human life is a great gift, that every part of it is designed by God and therefore means something, that every part of it is blessed by God and therefore to be enjoyed, that every part is accompanied by God and therefore workable.

We can't get away from God. He's there whether we like it or not, whether we know it or not. We can refuse to participate in God; we can act as if God weren't our designer, provider, and covenant presence. But when we refuse, we're less; our essential humanity is less. Our lives are diminished and impoverished.

LEAP OVER A WALL

GOOD AND JOYFUL

This great Message I delivered to you is
not mere human optimism. . . .
I got it straight . . . from Jesus Christ.

GALATIANS 1:11–12, THE MESSAGE

Paul discovered a personal relationship with God himself—no more secondhand rumor but firsthand faith. He immediately knew that God was not what he'd been told at all—that was all a lie. God was not *against* but *for*. God was not furious but compassionate. God was not out to get sinners so that he could make them good and sorry; he was out to get sinners so that he could make them good and joyful. This truth about God came to Paul in the person of God's son, Jesus Christ.

TRAVELING LIGHT

LIVING IN WHOLENESS

Live . . . a life Jesus will be proud of: bountiful in fruits from the soul. . . .

PHILIPPIANS 1:10–11, THE MESSAGE

Christian spirituality means living in the mature wholeness of the gospel. It means taking all the elements of your life—children, spouse, job, weather, possessions, relationships— and experiencing them as an act of faith. God wants all the material of our lives. . . .

The assumption of spirituality is that always God is doing something before I know it. So the task is not to get God to do something I think needs to be done, but to become aware of what God is doing so I can respond to it and participate and take delight in it.

THE CONTEMPLATIVE PASTOR

THE REASON FOR PRAYER

Let my cry come right into your presence, GOD.

PSALM 119:170, THE MESSAGE

The Psalms were not prayed by people trying to understand themselves. They are not the record of people searching for the meaning of life. They were prayed by people who understood that God had everything to do with them. God, not their feelings, was the center. God, not their souls, was the issue. God, not the meaning of life, was critical.

Feelings, souls, and meanings were not excluded—they are very much in evidence—but they are not the reason for the prayers. Human experiences might provoke the prayers, but they do not condition them *as* prayers.

ANSWERING GOD

GOD'S WORD, NOT OURS

He spoke, and it came to be;
he commanded, and it stood forth.

PSALM 33:9, RSV

The word of God constitutes the total reality in which we find ourselves. Everything we see and feel and deal with—sea and sky, codfish and warblers, sycamores and carrots—originates by means of this word. Everything, absolutely everything, was *spoken* into being. The *word* is as foundational in the work of salvation as it is in the work of creation. Just as everything outside us originates in the word of God, so does everything inside us.

Everywhere we look, everywhere we probe, everywhere we listen we come upon *word*—and it is God's word, not ours.

WORKING THE ANGLES

LOVE IS A DECISION

Love means following his commandments,
and his unifying commandment
is that you conduct your lives in love.

2 JOHN 6, THE MESSAGE

[A
gape love] is not first of all a feeling, or an experience, or a need, but a decision. It wills the fulfillment of the other. It is the love that is demonstrated by God for His people. It is a love that neither exploits needs nor demands gifts. It seeks to enjoy what is there in the other person and to share what one has. It is the love that Jesus exhibited in every word and act.

His love freed others to be themselves in a way they could never have been without Him and allowed them to respond with a love for God that no sense of dependence or realization of duty could have created.

LIKE DEW YOUR YOUTH

LIVING GOD-WARDS

The moment I called out, you stepped in;
you made my life large with strength.

PSALM 138:3, THE MESSAGE

One of the first things that strikes us about the men and women in Scripture is that they were disappointingly nonheroic. . . . Abraham lied; Jacob cheated; Moses murdered and complained; David committed adultery; Peter blasphemed. . . .

[Yet] the persons we meet on the pages of Scripture are remarkable for the intensity with which they live God-wards, the thoroughness in which all the details of their lives are included in God's word to them, in God's action in them. It is these persons, who are conscious of participating in what God is saying and doing, who are most human, most alive.

RUN WITH THE HORSES

DOUBT AND FAITH

The person who lives in right relationship with God does it by embracing what God arranges for him.

GALATIANS 3:11, THE MESSAGE

The claim of the gospel is that it puts us in touch with reality—all of it, not just a part. It puts us in touch with a God who creates and with the people and world he created. It puts us in touch with a Christ who redeems and the people whom he loves. It puts us in touch with our feelings of hope and despair, with our thoughts of doubt and faith, with our acts of virtue and vice. It puts us in touch with everything, visible and invisible, right and wrong, good and evil. It puts us in touch and then trains us in mature ways of living.

TRAVELING LIGHT

WE EXPECT MERCY

We're watching and waiting, holding our breath,
awaiting your word of mercy.

PSALM 123:2, THE MESSAGE

What happens when we look up to God in faith? There is an awesome mystery in God that we can never completely penetrate. We cannot define God; we cannot package God. But that doesn't mean that we are completely at sea with God, never knowing what to expect, nervously on edge all the time, wondering what he might do.

We know very well what to expect, and what we expect is mercy.

A LONG OBEDIENCE

SINGLENESS OF FOCUS

God, the one and only—I'll wait as long as he says.

PSALM 62:1, THE MESSAGE

God is not one among many. When we pray we are not covering our bases. Prayer is not a way of checking out a last resort of potential help. We understandably want to explore all the options: we write letters, make telephone calls, visit prospects, arrange interviews. We don't know who might be useful to us at any one time. Of course, we cultivate God. But not in prayer. We try it, but it doesn't work.

Prayer is exclusive. Prayer is centering. . . . We can't pray with one eye on the main chance and a side glance for God. Prayer trains the soul to singleness of focus: for God *alone*.

WHERE YOUR TREASURE IS

ROBUST IN PRAISE

God always does what he says,
and is gracious in everything he does.

PSALM 145:13, THE MESSAGE

David was a master at asking God for what he needed. Bold and eloquent in his asking—asking for help, for refuge, for healing, for salvation, for deliverance, for forgiveness, for mercy, for the Holy Spirit. He was also wonderfully robust in praise, but the praise was all mined from this hardscrabble life of asking.

LEAP OVER A WALL

PRAYER IN OUR STORY

Christ brought you over to God's side and put your lives together, whole and holy in his presence.

COLOSSIANS 1:22, THE MESSAGE

Everyone's life is [filled with] conflict and failure and fear, love and betrayal, loss and salvation. Every day is a story, a morning beginning and evening ending that are boundaries for people who go about their tasks with more or less purpose, go to war, make love, earn a living, scheme and sin and believe. Everything is connected. Meaning is everywhere. The days add up to a life that is a story. . . .

All prayer is prayed in a story, by someone who is in the story. . . . Prayers are prayed by people who live stories.

ANSWERING GOD

GOD'S INTENT

I inherited your book on living; it's mine forever
—what a gift!

PSALM 119:111, THE MESSAGE

Apart from Scripture there are guessed-at relationships between God and his creatures, surmised anticipations of God's intent, conjectures and speculations on God's nature and ways of working. But in the pages of Scripture we see the acts of salvation, of providence, of blessing.

God's word brings creation into being, brings people into existence. We see God bridging the abyss of sin and establishing peace. We see God disciplining and nurturing rebellious and recalcitrant people to the end that love can be experienced and developed to maturity. We see God entering our history in the form of a servant so that we can freely participate in the redemption that God is working in us.

REVERSED THUNDER

FREE CHOICE

Be generous with me and I'll live a full life;
not for a minute will I take my eyes off your road.

PSALM 119:17, THE MESSAGE

Christians are not determinists. We do not believe that environment makes a person a Christian, and we do not believe that heredity makes a person righteous. We do not believe that training can make a person moral, and we do not believe that baptism can create a person of faith. Christian theology maintains that every person makes his or her own decisions for or against God.

Every life is an accumulation of such decisions. No one can choose right for another. The choice is free. The decision is open. Anyone, regardless of background and upbringing, can choose either way. "Multitudes, multitudes, in the valley of decision!" (Joel 3:14, RSV)

LIKE DEW YOUR YOUTH

THE WAY OF FAITH

Keep your eyes on Jesus, who both
began and finished this race we're in.

HEBREWS 12:2, THE MESSAGE

W hen mountain climbers are in dangerous terrain. . . they rope themselves together. Sometimes one of them slips and falls—backslides. But not everyone falls at once, and so those who are still on their feet are able to keep the backslider from falling away completely. And of course, in any group of climbers there is a veteran climber in the lead, indentified for us in the letter to the Hebrews as "Jesus, who both began and finished this race we're in."

Traveling in the way of faith and climbing the ascent to Christ may be difficult, but it is not worrisome. The weather may be adverse, but it is never fatal. We may slip and stumble and fall, but the rope will hold us.

A LONG OBEDIENCE

GOD'S PROMISES

"I am watching over my word to perform it."

JEREMIAH 1:12, RSV

The almond tree is one of the earliest trees to bloom in Palestine. Before it puts forth leaves, it puts forth blossoms, white and snowy. While the land is still chill from winter, the warm blossoms, untended and unforced, surprise us with a promise of spring. Every spring it happens again. . . .

The blossom is a delight in itself, . . . fragrant to smell. But it is more. It is anticipation. It is promise. Like words. . . . God's words. . . . They are promises that lead to fulfillment. . . . God does what he says.

RUN WITH THE HORSES

GLORY IN DIVERSITY

There is neither Jew nor Greek, there is neither
slave nor free, there is neither male
nor female; for you are all one in Christ Jesus.

GALATIANS 3:28, RSV

All the children in a family are different—different sizes, different states of health, different temperaments. . . . And the parent deals with each differently. But the same love and wisdom is exercised in relation to each. We at our best (and we not always are) do not have favorite children. God at his best (and he always is) does not have favorite children.

How freeing it is to discover that! Other people then are no longer a threat to our security or our chances of being recognized and loved. We are not rivals competing for a prize, but participants in a common life, brothers and sisters in a single family. We are free to accept, even glory in, our diversity.

TRAVELING LIGHT

FAILURE AND FAITH

God's readiness to give and forgive is now public. Salvation's available for everyone!

TITUS 2:11, THE MESSAGE

Michelangelo sculpted in marble what many Jews and Christians have carved in their imaginations—a flawless David, the spirited human body in perfection. But the biblical text does not give us a flawless David. Putting people on pedestals is a way of not having to deal with who they really are (and who the God working in them really is).

The biblical narrator insists on telling us everything bad about David. . . . The narrator refuses to idealize or glamorize him to show that God's sovereignty works through just such a mixed bag of human failure and sin.

"BATHSHEBA-GATE," CHRISTIANITY TODAY

FREE TO LOVE

Love others as you love yourself.
That's an act of true freedom.

GALATIANS 5:14, THE MESSAGE

Each person is God's person, standing before God as his child and before me as a brother or sister. "All men," wrote William Law, "are great instances of divine love, therefore let all men be instances of your love."

This person does not stand before me as an obstruction or a threat or an affront. If I cannot see the person in relation to God, then I am not free to love. I will either want to get rid of her because she is in my way, or I will want to use her in order to get my own way. Either way I lose freedom.

TRAVELING LIGHT

REMEMBER AND RECEIVE

Then he took a cup, and . . .
said to them, "This is my blood of the covenant,
which is poured out for many."

MARK 14:23–24, NRSV

The eucharistic meal . . . is the primary way that Christians remember, receive, and share the meaning of our salvation: Christ crucified for us, his blood shed for the remission of our sins. This is where we affirm the action of our salvation.

The many-dimensioned reality of salvation is preserved not by a truth that we must figure out, or by an ethical behavior that we must carry out, but in a meal to eat. Not everyone can comprehend a doctrine; not everyone can obey a precept; but everyone can eat a piece of bread, drink a cup of wine, and understand a simple statement—my body, my blood.

REVERSED THUNDER

POSSIBILITIES

The sufferings of this present time are not
worthy to be compared with
the glory which shall be revealed in us.

ROMANS 8:18, NKJV

The Bible spends only a few pages establishing the conditions of our beginnings; and then several hundred pages cultivating in us a taste for the future—immersing us in a narrative in which the future is always impinging on the present. . . .

The future is not a blank to be filled in, depending on our mood, by either fantasy or horror, but a source of brightness that we await and receive. Our lives are still outstanding. Our prayers give expression to lives that go far beyond the past and present and reach into what is promised and prophesied. When we pray we can no loner confine our understanding of ourselves to who we are or have been; we understand ourselves in terms of possibilities yet to be realized.

ANSWERING GOD

RULED BY GOD

I am about to do a new thing;
now it springs forth, do you not perceive it?

ISAIAH 43:19, NRSV

The gospel message says: "You don't live in a mechanistic world ruled by necessity; you don't live in a random world ruled by chance; you live in a world ruled by the God of Exodus and Easter. He will do things in you that neither you nor your friends would have supposed possible. He is not limited by anything you think you know about him; he is not boxed into the cramped dimensions of your ignorance or your despair. As Isaiah says, 'I am about to do a new thing.'"

FIVE SMOOTH STONES

FEBRUARY

In prayer
we do not act,
God does.

TRUE LISTENING

"I'll live in them, move into them;
I'll be their God and they'll be my people."

2 CORINTHIANS 6:14, THE MESSAGE

Persons in love often describe . . . their new relationship in some such words as, "for the first time in my life I can say everything I feel and think." This is not because they have added new words to their vocabulary or because they have taken speech lessons. It is because they have met someone who listens. True speaking is made possible when there is true listening. What good are words without a listener?

God listens. Everything we say, every groan, every murmur, every stammering attempt at prayer: all this is listened to.

We are listened to. We realize dignity. . . . We acquire hope.

REVERSED THUNDER

GOD IS THE CENTER

*Like an open book, you watched me
grow from conception to birth; all the stages
of my life were spread out before you.*

PSALM 139:16, THE MESSAGE

No child is just a child. Each is a creature in whom God intends to do something glorious and great. No one is only a product of the genes contributed by parents. Who we are and will be is compounded with who God is and what he does. . . .

Our lives are not puzzles to be figured out. Rather, we come to God, who knows us and reveals to us the truth of our lives. The fundamental mistake is to begin with ourselves and not God. God is the center from which all life develops.

RUN WITH THE HORSES

RULED BY GOD

GOD guards you from every evil,
he guards your very life.

PSALM 121:7, THE MESSAGE

Christians travel the same ground that everyone else walks on, breathe the same air, drink the same water, shop in the same stores, read the same newspapers, are citizens under the same governments, pay the same prices for groceries and gasoline, fear the same dangers, are subject to the same pressures, get the same distresses, are buried in the same ground.

The difference is that each step we walk, each breath we breathe, we know we are ruled by God; and therefore no matter what doubts we endure or what accidents we experience, the Lord will guard us from every evil. He guards our very life.

A LONG OBEDIENCE

DESIGN AND ORDER

*It's wonderful what happens when
Christ displaces worry at the center of your life.*

PHILIPPIANS 4:7, THE MESSAGE

L ife is not a haphazard affair run by a
committee that meets on alternate Tuesdays,
each member subject to intense lobbying by
special interests and prone to play favorites with
friends and family. The world has design and
order. I can plan, hope, believe. The confusion and
conflict that convulse history are bounded by a
larger clarity and peace.

WHERE YOUR TREASURE IS

TELLING STORIES

I tell stories: to create readiness,
to nudge the people toward receptive insight.

MATTHEW 13:13, THE MESSAGE

Story is the primary way in which the revelation of God is given to us. . . . Moses told stories; Jesus told stories; the four Gospel writers presented their good news in the form of stories. . . .

The reason that story is so basic to us is that life itself has a narrative shape—a beginning and end, plot and characters, conflict and resolution. Life isn't an accumulation of abstractions such as love and truth, sin and salvation . . . ; life is the realization of details that all connect . . . : names and fingerprints, street numbers, . . . lamb for supper. God reveals himself to us . . . in the kind of stories we use to tell our children who they are and how to grow up as human beings.

LEAP OVER A WALL

SURPRISING GOOD NEWS

You're the preacher of good news.
Speak loud and clear. Don't be timid!

ISAIAH 40:9, THE MESSAGE

Good tidings. Good news. Gospel.

This gospel is not just any good news— not the good news of a pay raise, or of a good grade in school, or of the victory of our favorite athletic team, or of the happy solution to some international problem. It is the unexpected, fresh, surprising good news that God loves and has provided the means for our salvation. That love and that salvation are at the center of absolutely everything, and from that center all of life is lived. This word has nothing to do with the hopeful, brave, encouraging words we use to bolster each other through hard times and cheer one another on. It is good news about *God.*

TRAVELING LIGHT

A DOCTRINE OF GOD

Thank GOD for his marvelous love,
for his miracle mercy to the children he loves.

PSALM 107:31, THE MESSAGE

It is not possible to comprehend God. Merely to utter the name "God" is to be plunged into mystery. But that doesn't mean that we are in the dark, where all cats are gray. At least it did not for the Hebrews, or the praying Christians in their train.

None of them knew very much about God, but they knew a few things with clarity. . . . They had a *doctrine* of God. Some things were true: Adamic creation, Abrahamic covenant, Exodus salvation, Mosaic commands. Some things were not true: God was not arbitrary, not destructive, not indifferent.

ANSWERING GOD

A BROAD PLACE

I called on the LORD in distress; the LORD answered me, and set me in a broad place.

PSALM 118:5, NKJV

Salvation means to be whole again, to be delivered in the midst of peril. Far back toward the Hebrew root of the word, it may even suggest that no matter how closely the evil hedges you about, God will yet clear for you all the space you need to move around in: "I called on the LORD in distress: the LORD answered me, *and set me* in a broad place."

FIVE SMOOTH STONES

DAY TO NIGHT

I stretch myself out. I sleep.
Then I'm up again—rested, tall and steady.

PSALM 3:5, THE MESSAGE

Day is the basic unit of God's creative work; evening is the beginning of that day. It is the onset of God speaking light, stars, earth . . . into being. But it is also the time when we quit our activity and go to sleep. . . .

The day is about to begin! God's genesis words are about to be spoken again. During the hours of my sleep, how will he prepare to use my obedience, service, and speech when morning breaks? I go to sleep to get out of the way for awhile. I get into the rhythm of salvation.

WORKING THE ANGLES

CREATIVITY IS MESSY

Knowing what is right is like deep water in the heart; a wise person draws from the well within.

PROVERBS 20:5, THE MESSAGE

Creativity is not neat. It is not orderly. When we are being creative we don't know what is going to happen next. When we are being creative a great deal of what we do is wrong. . . .

An artist makes attempt after attempt at the canvas trying for the right perspective and missing badly, almost getting the right shade but not making it. . . . Lovers quarrel, hurt and get hurt, misunderstand and are misunderstood in their painstaking work of creating a marriage. . . .

In any creative enterprise there are risks, mistakes, . . . but out of this mess—when we stay with it long enough, enter it deeply enough— there slowly emerges love or beauty or peace.

UNDER THE UNPREDICTABLE PLANT

THE DRAMA OF REDEMPTION

God is greater than our worried hearts
and knows more about us than we do ourselves.

1 JOHN 3:21, THE MESSAGE

I n Jesus the word of God became a matter of personal response between sinful people and a loving Savior. What mattered was that people respond: the inner life of faith, hope, confession, and repentance was called into being. The heart—that great biblical metaphor for all that makes us function in relation to God—is the site for the action.

Religion is not a ritual in which some act out the truths for others, but a faith in which each person experiences what God has for her or him. All the great dramas of redemption are acted out, not on a Greek stage, but in a human heart.

LIKE DEW YOUR YOUTH

MY PLACE IN LIFE

Blessed GOD! His love is the wonder of the world.

PSALM 31:22, THE MESSAGE

With God I am not a zero. Not a minus. I have a set-apart place that only I can fill. No one can substitute for me. No one can replace me. Before I was good for anything, God decided that I was good for what he was doing. My place in life doesn't depend on how well I do in the entrance examination. My place in life is not determined by what market there is for my type of personality.

God is out to win the world in love and each person has been selected to . . . do it with him.

RUN WITH THE HORSES

FREEDOM

Christ has set us free to live a free life.

GALATIANS 5:1, THE MESSAGE

Among the apostles, the one absolutely stunning success was Judas, and the one thoroughly groveling failure was Peter. Judas was a success in the ways that most impress us: he was successful both financially and politically. . . . And Peter was a failure in ways that we most dread: he was impotent in a crisis and socially inept. . . .

Time, of course, has reversed our judgements on the two men. Judas is now a byword for betrayal, and Peter is one of the most honored names in church and world. . . . Yet the world continues to chase after the successes of Judas, financial wealth and political power, and to defend itself against the failures of Peter, impotence and ineptness. But anyone who has learned the first thing about freedom prefers to fail with Peter than to succeed with Judas.

TRAVELING LIGHT

GOD IS THE POTTER

Oh, blessed be GOD! He didn't go off and leave us.

PSALM 124:6, THE MESSAGE

The basic conviction of a Christian is that God intends good for us and that he will get his way in us. He does not treat us according to our deserts, but according to his plan. He is not a police officer on patrol, watching over the universe, ready to club us if we get out of hand or put us in jail if we get obstreperous. He is a potter working with the clay of our lives, forming and reforming until, finally, he has shaped a redeemed life, a vessel fit for a kingdom.

A LONG OBEDIENCE

MY SOUL WAITS

For God alone my soul waits in silence,
for my hope is from him.

PSALM 62:5, RSV

My soul waits. Another will is greater, wiser and more intelligent than my own. So I wait. Waiting means there is another whom I trust and from whom I receive. My will, important and essential as it is, finds a will that is more important, more essential. . . .

I begin to pray by attempting to manipulate the will of God. I end by putting myself in a position to be moved by his will. Waiting in prayer is a disciplined refusal to act before God acts.

WHERE YOUR TREASURE IS

WE NEED GOD

Put your hope in GOD and know real blessing!

PSALM 146:5, THE MESSAGE

We're aware of something we need or lack most of the time. We're not complete. We're not fully human. This sense of being unfinished is pervasive and accounts for a great deal that's distinctive in us as humans. We then attempt to complete ourselves by getting more education or more money, going to another place or buying different clothes, searching out new experiences. The Christian gospel tells us that in and under and around all of these incompletions is God: God is who we need. The God-hunger, the God-thirst is the most powerful drive in us. It's far stronger than all the drives of sex, power, security, and fame put together.

LEAP OVER A WALL

VERY GOD, VERY MAN

As the lightning comes from the east
and flashes as far as the west, so will be the
coming of the Son of Man.

MATTHEW 24:27, NRSV

Jesus was systematic in this double affirmation: he was, in fact, Son of Man "given dominion and glory and kingdom"; he was, in fact, completely at home in the ordinary, the everyday, the common. He did not give an inch in either direction: he was very God, very man.

The task of faith, for those who agreed to be his disciples, was to accept the literal truth of the title Son of Man under such conditions, to immerse themselves in cross-bearing, self-denial, suffering, and death at the same time they believed that everything they did or spoke was part of the victorious rule of God's kingdom.

REVERSED THUNDER

THE JESUS-REVEALED LIFE

*He used his servant body to carry our sins to the Cross
so we could be rid of sin, free to live the right way.*

1 PETER 2:24, THE MESSAGE

Those years of association with Jesus for the
disciples, years of "growing up," were years
of realizing in sharp and precise detail that life
is what God gives us in Jesus: grace, healing,
forgiveness, deliverance from evil, a miraculous
meal, the personal presence and word of God.
And now that they know what it is, they know it
is *not* self-preservation, self-help, self-aggrandizement,
self-importance.

Life is the Jesus revealed life that becomes
plain as day on the cross—the sacrificial life, the
life that loves generously and extravagantly, the life
that through voluntary and sacrificial death to self
becomes resurrection for the world.

LIKE DEW YOUR YOUTH

WE ANSWER GOD

Listen while I build my case, GOD,
the most honest prayer you'll ever hear.

PSALM 17:1, THE MESSAGE

Miqra, the Hebrew word for Bible, properly means "calling out"—the calling out of God to us. "God must become a person," but in order for us to speak in answer to him he must make us into persons. We become ourselves as we answer, sometimes angrily disputing with him about how he rules the world, sometimes humbling ourselves before him in grateful trust. . . .

In prayer we do not merely speak our feelings, we speak our answers. We can answer; we are permitted to answer. If we truly answer God there is nothing that we may not say to him.

ANSWERING GOD

GOD GIVES JOY

All things work together
for good to those who love God.

ROMANS 8:28, NKJV

One of the most interesting and remarkable things Christians learn is that laughter does not exclude weeping. Christian joy is not an escape from sorrow. Pain and hardship still come, but they are unable to drive out the happiness of the redeemed. . . .

Joy is what God gives, not what we work up. Laughter is the delight that things are working together for good to those who love God, . . . an overflow of spirits that comes from feeling good not about yourself but about God.

A Long Obedience

GOD ACCOMPLISHES GOOD

Show me how you work, GOD;
school me in your ways.

PSALM 25:4, THE MESSAGE

We cannot afford to be naïve about evil—it must be faced. But we cannot be intimidated by it either. It will be used by God to bring good. For it is one of the most extraordinary aspects of the good news that God uses bad men to accomplish his good purposes. . . .

If we forget that the newspapers are footnotes to Scripture and not the other way around, we will finally be afraid to get out of bed in the morning. Too many of us spend far too much time with the editorial page. . . . We get our interpretation of politics and economics and morals from journalists when we should be getting only information. The *meaning* of the world is most accurately given to us by God's Word.

RUN WITH THE HORSES

FAITH AND FREEDOM

Grace . . . invites us into life—a life that
goes on and on and on, world without end.

ROMANS 5:21, THE MESSAGE

We are not free from failure. We find that the good intentions of our parents have not always worked out for the good. . . . We find that our teachers were not always honest and that our minds therefore have distorted and inadequate ideas. . . . We find that we want to be good, to be whole, and that we are not. . . . We realize we are not free for what we want most of all—to be complete.

We are free to do many things. We are free from many restrictions. But what about the center? What about God? *There* we live by faith and failure, by faith and forgiveness, by faith and mercy, by faith and freedom.

Traveling Light

WE NEED GOD

The LORD looks down from heaven upon the children of men, to see if there are any that act wisely, that seek after God.

PSALM 14:2, RSV

We need God under our feet and God in our lungs. . . . God is the great continent of reality on which we live. If we deny him in practice by attempting to live in the ocean of the self, we are soon fatigued and require all kinds of artificial aids to keep us afloat—pieces of driftwood, life jackets. It is not our proper environment. We are forever getting our lungs full of water, getting rescued, receiving artificial respiration. Then we go out and start it all over again.

Why don't we simply come out of the ocean of the self and stand on our own two feet on the dry land of the kingdom of God?

WHERE YOUR TREASURE IS

A MORAL MAELSTROM

*Live out this God-created identity
the way our Father lives toward us, generously and
graciously, even when we're at our worst.*

LUKE 6:35, THE MESSAGE

We Christians should be well trained through our Bible reading to see how God's sovereignty is worked out through the lives of frail, willful, disobedient—sometimes repentant and sometimes not—men and women who are created to live to God's glory. *That* is what keeps us reading this story over and over again and finding it "good news."

In the moral maelstrom of our age, people ask, "How do we keep our moral equilibrium with stories [about people with questionable lifestyles] in the middle of our Bibles?" and the answer is this: "By keeping them in the middle of our Bibles."

"BATHSHEBA-GATE," CHRISTIANITY TODAY

INCREASINGLY FREE

The whole law is fulfilled in one word,
"You shall love your neighbor as yourself."

GALATIANS 5:14, RSV

"The whole law is fulfilled," says Paul, "through love."

Grammatically, the word *fulfilled* is in the perfect tense. As such it means the whole law has been fulfilled every time one person loves another as himself.

To love my neighbors as less than myself is to treat them as a means to my ends. To love them as more would set them up for using me as a means to their ends. One way is as much a violation of love as the other, and as destructive of freedom. The command protects my freedom as much as yours, yours as much as mine. No one sacrifices freedom at the expense of the other. All become increasingly free.

TRAVELING LIGHT

COMMON WORSHIP

Applause, everyone. Bravo, bravissimo!
Shout God-songs at the top of your lungs!

PSALM 47:1, THE MESSAGE

In worship the community of God's people assemble to hear God's word spoken in scripture, sermon, and sacrament. The faith that is created by that proclaimed word develops responses of praise, obedience, and commitment.

At no time has there ever been a biblical faith or any kind of continuing life in relation to God, apart from such common worship. By persisting in the frequent, corporate worship in which God's word is central, God's people are prevented from making up a religion out of their own private ideas of God.

FIVE SMOOTH STONES

LOVE IS A LARGE WORD

How exquisite your love, O God!

PSALM 36:7, THE MESSAGE

The Hebrew word *chesed*, narrowly translated as "love," is a large word. No single word in our language is adequate to translate it, so we revert to the use of adjectives to bring out the distinctive quality and broad reach of this love: steadfast love, loyal love. . . .

Chesed is often used in biblical revelation to designate God's love. But we humans, who have been created in the image of God, are also capable of loving this way, even though we never seem to get very good at it. *Chesed* is love without regard to shifting circumstances, hormones, emotional states, and personal convenience.

LEAP OVER A WALL

DISCERNING GRACE

Stay wide-awake in prayer.

1 PETER 4:7, THE MESSAGE

Feelings are real, and they are important. But they are real and important in the same way that our fingernails and noses are important—we would not want to live without them (although we could if we had to), but their length and shape and color tell us nothing about life with God.

To suppose that our emotions in any way give us reliable evidence of the nature or quality of our life with God is to misinterpret them. They are wonderful and necessary and glorious. They are part of the rich and stunning complexity of the human being in the image of God. We must value and develop and share them. But they are not prayer. All the spiritual masters are careful to guide us in a detachment from our feelings as a means for discerning grace or guiding prayer.

ANSWERING GOD

*All work is
participation in the
divine work.*

LET US NOT GROW WEARY

*Let us not grow weary in well-doing, for
in due season we shall reap, if we do not lose heart.*

GALATIANS 6:9, RSV

E very word of encouragement, every prayer of
intercession, every act of helping is seed that
will mature to eternal life. . . .

The person, though, who looks for quick
results in the seed planting of well-doing will be
disappointed. If I want potatoes for dinner
tomorrow, it will do me little good to go out and
plant potatoes in my garden tonight. There are
long stretches of darkness and invisibility and
silence that separate planting and reaping. During
the stretches of waiting there is cultivating and
weeding and nurturing and planting still other
seeds. "Let us not grow weary in well-doing." The
task is endless.

TRAVELING LIGHT

CORONATION ON A CROSS

The kingdom of the world has become the kingdom of our Lord . . . and he shall reign for ever and ever.

REVELATION 11:15, RSV

Jesus announced the presence of the Kingdom of God. The word was often on his lips. At the end, he accepted the title King in that kingdom. He clearly intended that everyone know that the rule of God was comprehensive, established over body as well as soul, over society as well as individuals. . . .

He just as clearly repudiated the accustomed means by which that rule was exercised: he rejected the devil's offer of a position in government, rebuked the brothers Boanerges for wanting to call down fire from heaven to incinerate their enemies, ordered Peter to put up his sword, and reassured Pilate that the governor's job was in no danger. Finally, to make sure no one missed the point, he arranged that his coronation take place on a cross.

REVERSED THUNDER

DISCIPLE AND PILGRIM

I am the way, and the truth, and the life.
No one comes to the Father except through me.

JOHN 14:5–6, NRSV

There are two biblical designations for people of faith that are extremely useful: *disciple* and *pilgrim*. Disciple *(mathetes)* says we are people who spend our lives apprenticed to our master, Jesus Christ. We are in a growing-learning relationship, always.

Pilgrim *(parepidemos)* tells us we are people who spend our lives going someplace, going to God, and whose path for getting there is the way, Jesus Christ. . . .

Jesus, answering Thomas's question . . . "How can we know the way?" gives us directions: "I am the way, and the truth, and the life."

A Long Obedience

DECLARATION OF AUTHORITY

This is my Son, the Beloved,
with whom I am well pleased.

MATTHEW 3:17, NRSV

The descent of the Holy Spirit in the form of a dove as Jesus rose from the waters [of baptism] was associated with the dove-delivered evidence of emergent life after the flood. God's blessing to Noah, which included a comprehensive delegation of authority, has a parallel in the heavenly voice to Jesus: "This is my Son, the Beloved." The phrase is a quotation from Psalm 2 and as such is not a term of endearment but a declaration of authority: Messiah emerges from the death-dealing abyss and rules over the chaos.

WHERE YOUR TREASURE IS

DEALING WITH GOD

You're the closest of all to me, GOD,
and all your judgments true.

PSALM 119:151, THE MESSAGE

We're never more alive than when we're dealing with God. And there's a sense in which we aren't alive at all (in the uniquely human sense of "alive") *until* we're dealing with God.

David deals with God. As an instance of humanity in himself, he isn't much. He has little wisdom to pass on to us about how to live successfully. He was an unfortunate parent and an unfaithful husband. From a purely historical point of view he was a barbaric chieftain with a talent for poetry. But David's importance isn't in his mortality or his military prowess but in his experience of and witness to God. Every event in his life was confrontation with God.

LEAP OVER A WALL

GOD SETS THINGS RIGHT

You call out to God for help and he helps.

1 PETER 1:17, THE MESSAGE

Someone says, "Listen, God doesn't have time for your little problems. He is busy in the Middle East right now. He has bigger fish to fry. If you want something for yourself, you better get it the best way you can: buy this product and you will be important; wear these clothes and everyone will realize how distinguished you are. . . ."

The only good news that will make a difference is that the living God personally addresses and mercifully forgives us. He sets things right at the center. That is what we need, what we want.

TRAVELING LIGHT

PAYING ATTENTION TO GOD

We bless GOD, oh yes—we bless him now,
we bless him always!

PSALM 115:18, THE MESSAGE

Prayer is the most thoroughly *present* act we have as humans, and the most energetic: it sockets the immediate past into the immediate future and makes a flexible, living joint of them. The Amen gathers what has just happened into the Maranatha of the about to happen and produces a Benediction. We pay attention to God and lead others to pay attention to God. It hardly matters that so many people would rather pay attention to their standards of living, or their self-image, or their zeal to make a mark in the world.

The reality is God: worship or flee.

THE CONTEMPLATIVE PASTOR

CROSS OF DISCIPLESHIP

*Stay on good terms with
each other, held together by love.*

HEBREWS 13:1, THE MESSAGE

Writing cheerful graffiti on the rocks in the valley of deep shadows is no substitute for companionship with the person who must walk in the darkness.

The gospel that boldly sets the cross of Christ at the center of its message also courageously accepts the cross of discipleship as part of its daily routines. Difficulties and suffering are not problems for which the gospel provides an escape, but part of a reality that the Christian experiences and in which Christians share a faith by encouraging one another in hope.

FIVE SMOOTH STONES

KEEPING SABBATH

In six days God made Heaven, Earth, and sea,
and everything in them; he rested on the seventh day.

EXODUS 20:11, THE MESSAGE

I n the two biblical versions of the Sabbath commandment, the commands are identical but the supporting reasons differ. The Exodus reason is that we are to keep a Sabbath because God kept it. . . .

The Deuteronomy reason for Sabbath-keeping is that our ancestors in Egypt went four hundred years without a vacation (Deut. 5:15). Never a day off. The consequence: they were no longer considered persons but slaves. Hands. Work units. Not persons created in the image of God but equipment for making bricks and building pyramids. . . .

Lest any of us do that to our neighbor or husband or wife or child or employee, we are commanded to keep a Sabbath.

WORKING THE ANGLES

DISCIPLES IN VOCATION

God cares about honesty in the workplace;
your business is his business.

PROVERBS 16:11, THE MESSAGE

The entire earth, not only geographically, but vocationally, has been the mission field for the Christian worker. If all this had been left only to "the religious," to ministers and missionaries, vast areas would have been neglected. Pastors and priests have had vital roles, but are neither more or less important than any other occupation in which individuals live out their discipleship in a vocation.

LIKE DEW YOUR YOUTH

WHAT WE DO BEST

You show your gratitude
through your generous offerings.

2 CORINTHIANS 9:12–13, THE MESSAGE

Birds have feet and can walk. Birds have talons and can grasp a branch securely. They can walk; they can cling. But *flying* is their characteristic action, and not until they fly are they living at their best, gracefully and beautifully.

Giving is what we do best. It is the air into which we were born. It is the action that was designed into us before our birth. *Giving* is the way the world is. God makes no exceptions for any of us. We are given away to our families, to our neighbors, to our friends, to our enemies—to the nations. Our life is for others. That is the way creation works.

RUN WITH THE HORSES

BOLDLY AND FREELY

I identified myself completely with him. . . .
I have been crucified with Christ.

GALATIANS 2:19, THE MESSAGE

Crucifixion ends one way of life and opens up another. It finishes a life in which the self is coddled and indulged and admired, and begins a life that is offered to God and raised as a living sacrifice.

Everything that Christ experienced we co-experience. Starting with Christ, the complete revelation of Christ in crucifixion and resurrection, we live extravagantly, boldly, and freely.

TRAVELING LIGHT

MAGNIFICATION OF GRACE

Thy way, O God, is holy.

PSALM 77:13, RSV

What happens in prayer is that an awareness develops: a lot more is going on in the world than I am conscious of when I am disappointed, or hurt, or frustrated, or embittered. . . .

Meditation is an intensification of awareness, of perception. When the focus of meditation is narrowly bound by feelings of self-pity, the self in isolation, the result is an intensification of misery. But if the focus is on God in the self, on God in history, on God in creation, the result is a magnification of grace: "Thy way, O God, is holy."

WHERE YOUR TREASURE IS

UNDER THE MERCY

Mercy, GOD, mercy!

PSALM 123:2, THE MESSAGE

"Mercy, GOD, mercy!" The prayer is not an attempt to get God to do what he is unwilling otherwise to do, but a reaching out to what we know that he does do, an expressed longing to receive what God is doing in and for us in Jesus Christ.

We live under the mercy. God does not treat us as alien others, lining us up so that he can evaluate our competence or our usefulness or our worth. He rules, guides, commands, loves us as children whose destinies he carries in his heart.

A LONG OBEDIENCE

SITTING BEFORE GOD

Then King David went in and sat before the LORD.

2 SAMUEL 7:18, RSV

D avid *sat.* This may be the single most critical act that David ever did, the action that put him out of action—more critical than killing Goliath, more critical than honoring Saul (his enemy) as God's anointed, more critical than bringing the Ark to Jerusalem.

By sitting down, David renounced royal initiative, abdicated kingly authority, got himself out of the driver's seat, and deliberately and reverently placed himself before God his King.

When David sat down before God, it was . . . trading in his plans for God's plans.

LEAP OVER A WALL

LIGHT IN OUR LIFE

God spoke: "Light!" And light appeared.

GENESIS 1:3, THE MESSAGE

The pre-Genesis condition of the cosmos is our own inner life—without form and void. Things are not right; *we* are not right. Our emotions bolt and stampede. Our thoughts run riot. Our bodies hurt. Our appetites play havoc with our virtue. We can't, it seems, direct our own destiny with dignity or wisdom for ten consecutive minutes.

And so we pray. Directed by the Psalms, we begin our praying by listening. What do we hear? "And God said, 'Let there be light.'"

Disorder gives way, piecemeal, to order. Chaos becomes cosmos.

ANSWERING GOD

RESPECT FOR GOD'S WORD

He brought us to life using the true Word,
showing us off as the crown of all his creatures.

JAMES 1:18, THE MESSAGE

Our capacity for language is the most distinctive thing about us as humans. Words are that by which we articulate who we are. Nothing about us is more significant than the way we use words. If words are used badly, our lives are debased.

The way we understand and become ourselves through the use of words has a corollary in how we understand God and his coming among us. The most distinctive feature of the Christian faith is its respect for the word: God's word first of all and secondarily our words of prayer, confession, and witness.

REVERSED THUNDER

RESHAPED BY OBEDIENCE

Don't quit in hard times; pray all the harder.

ROMANS 12:12, THE MESSAGE

Work is a major component in most lives. It is unavoidable. It can be either good or bad, an area where our sin is magnified or where our faith matures. For it is the nature of sin to take good things and twist them, ever so slightly, so that they miss the target to which they are aimed, the target of God. One requirement of discipleship is to learn the ways sin skews our nature and submit what we learn to the continuing will of God, so that we are reshaped through the days of our obedience.

A LONG OBEDIENCE

TRUST

"God is my salvation. I trust, I won't be afraid."

ISAIAH 12:2, THE MESSAGE

In order to be equipped to be what God calls us to be we need to know supremely these two subjects, God and world. In both subjects first impressions and surface appearances are deceiving. We underestimate God and we overestimate evil. We don't see what God is doing and conclude that he is doing nothing. We see everything that evil is doing and think it is in control of everyone.

If we are going to live in God's image, . . . we must trust in his word, trust what we do not see. And if we are going to live in the world, . . . we are going to have to face its immense evil, but know at the same time that it is a limited and controlled evil.

RUN WITH THE HORSES

GOD CARES

*We can't round up enough containers to hold
everything God generously pours
into our lives through the Holy Spirit!*

ROMANS 5:5, THE MESSAGE

We don't live by faith by reading a rule book, or following a map, or working through a career development program, or following the arrows. We do not begin with things, or pieces of paper, or ideas, or feelings, or deeds, or successes. We begin with God. We dare to believe that God cares who we are, knows who we are. We dare to believe that God is the reality beyond and beneath and around all things, visible and invisible, and that he provides for us and loves and blesses and saves us.

TRAVELING LIGHT

REVERENCE

Be subject to one another out of reverence for Christ.

EPHESIANS 5:21, RSV

Reverence is the operative word—*en pobo Christou*—awed, worshipful attentiveness, ready to respond in love and adoration. We do not learn our relationship with God out of a cocksure, arrogant knowledge of exactly what God wants. . . . Nor do we cower before him in a scrupulous anxiety that fears offending him. . . .

No. Gospel reverence, Christ reverence, is a vigorous (but by no means presumptuous) bold freedom, full of spontaneous energy. . . .

We are more than ready to bow down before Christ unafraid that we will be tyrannized, for Christ has already laid down his life for us on the cross, pouring himself out and holding nothing back.

THE CONTEMPLATIVE PASTOR

LONG LIFE OF LOVE

*A man leaves his father and mother
and embraces his wife. They become one flesh.*

GENESIS 2:24, THE MESSAGE

Every marriage introduces into society fresh energies of love and freedom that have the power to unself not only the lovers themselves but America itself. The mere introduction of these energies is not enough, however, or we would have become Utopia long since. They need continuing and perfecting. Where can we get that but in Christ? A prayed and praying faithfulness carries us into the long life of love in which and by which the world will not perish.

WHERE YOUR TREASURE IS

REALITY OF LIFE

If you seek GOD, your God, you'll be
able to find him if you're . . .
looking for him with your whole heart and soul.

DEUTERONOMY 4:29, THE MESSAGE

Normal life is full of distractions and irrelevancies. Then catastrophe: Illness. Accident. Job loss. Divorce. Death. The reality of our lives is rearranged without anyone consulting us or waiting for our permission. . . .

All of us are given moments, days, months, years of "exile." What will we do with them? Wish we were someplace else? Complain? Escape into fantasies? Drug ourselves into oblivion? Or build and plant and marry and seek the shalom of the place we inhabit and the people we are with? Exile reveals what really matters and frees us to pursue what really matters, which is to seek the Lord with all our hearts.

RUN WITH THE HORSES

WE WANT GOD

Mostly what God does is love you.
Keep company with him and learn a life of love.

EPHESIANS 5:1, THE MESSAGE

I t is God with whom we have to deal. People go for long stretches of time without being aware of that, thinking it is with money, or sex, or work, or children, or parents, or a political cause, or athletic competition, or learning that they must deal. Any one or a combination of these subjects can absorb them and give the meaning and purpose that human beings seem to require. But then there is a slow stretch of boredom. Or a disaster. Or a sudden collapse of meaning. They want more. They want God.

"LEADERSHIP JOURNAL"

LOVE IS FREEING

When we take up permanent residence in a
life of love, we live in God and God lives in us.

1 JOHN 4:16, THE MESSAGE

Love is the free act supreme. It directs our best intentions and our best abilities to the other. It marshals our best energies into companionship and friendship with a person whom God has singled out for love. The act is not controlled by feelings or circumstances, by prejudices or customs. We are free to love the person who is presented as an enemy, the person who is designated as insignificant, the person who apparently has nothing of interest or worth to me, the person who insists on making himself unpleasant to me.

It is a great freedom to love. It means the freedom to be myself, uniquely, totally, and affirmatively with this other.

TRAVELING LIGHT

GOD OF POWER

His generosity never gives out
. . . this GOD of Grace, this GOD of love.

PSALM 111:3–4, THE MESSAGE

There's much to fear in life. We constantly meet up with people who have more power than we have. How will they use that power, that authority? Will they diminish us, exploit us, use us, get rid of us? We learn to be cautious, put up defenses.

And then we come before God, a God of power and mystery. How will he treat us? Will he punish us, destroy us, take away our freedom? Based on our experience, any of that is certainly possible, maybe even probable. That's why we need so much reassurance: "Relax. It's going to be all right."

LEAP OVER A WALL

LOVING OTHERS

"Love others as well as you love yourself."

MATTHEW 22:40, THE MESSAGE

The Bible knows nothing of a religion defined by what a person does inwardly in the privacy of thought or feeling, or apart from others on lonely retreat. When Jesus was asked what the great commandment was, he said, "Love the Lord your God with all your passion and prayer and intelligence." Then immediately, before anyone could go off and make a private religion out of it ("I come to the garden alone"), riveted it to another: "There is a second to set alongside it: 'Love others as well as you love yourself.'"

A Long Obedience

A LARGE GENEROSITY

Thank GOD! Pray to him by name!
Tell everyone you meet what he has done!

PSALM 105:1, THE MESSAGE

The Psalms that teach us to pray never leave us to ourselves; they embed all our prayers in liturgy. . . .

Liturgy pulls our prayers out of the tiresome business of looking after ourselves and into the exhilarating enterprise of seeing and participating in what God is doing. We are drawn into a large generosity where everyone is getting and receiving, offering and praising. We are drawn to the place where people are being loved and where they love us.

ANSWERING GOD

JOY IN COMMUNITY

"I have said these things to you so that my joy may be in you, and that your joy may be full."

JOHN 15:11, NRSV

Salvation is not only individual; it is corporate. In the corporateness, and because of it, there is joy. Joy is not a private emotion; it requires community for both its development and expression. And since the community is provided and preserved by God, the response is joy in God. . . .

Joy, separated from its roots in God and pursued apart from the community of faith, becomes mere sensation. It is as easy to separate experiences of joy from God as it is to separate experiences of suffering from God. If the result of the latter is bitterness, the result of the former is boredom.

FIVE SMOOTH STONES

GOD RUNS THE COSMOS

In his right hand he held seven stars.

REVELATION 1:16, NRSV

Christ holds the seven stars in his right hand! "Right hand" means ready for use. A soldier with a sword in his right hand is ready to fight; a shepherd with a staff in the right hand is at work; a hammer in the right hand is ready to pound a sixpenny nail into a loose floorboard. What is in my right hand is what I am capable of doing and what, in fact, I am ready to do. What does Christ do? He runs the cosmos. It is that simple. The planets do not control us; Christ controls the planets.

REVERSED THUNDER

COUNTRY OF FREEDOM

If the Son makes you free, you will be free indeed.

JOHN 8:36, RSV

We commit ourselves to a living Christ and discover that we are introduced into the country of freedom. We receive into ourselves the gift-bringing Spirit and realize the aptitudes and abilities for living freely. Apart from faith in God we live in a world of brute determinism, bullied by those who are stronger than we. . . . Or, we live in an absurd, haphazard randomness.

In faith we find ourselves in a . . . developing relationship with a free God and therefore able to experience and realize freedom ourselves. . . .

TRAVELING LIGHT

APRIL

We are created

to adore.

A FRESH CANVAS

You know exactly how I was made, bit by bit,
how I was sculpted from nothing into something.

PSALM 139:15, THE MESSAGE

We find that Scripture is sparing in the information it gives on people while it is lavish in what it tells us about God. It refuses to feed our lust for hero worship. It will not pander to our adolescent desire to join a fan club. The reason is . . . clear enough. Fan clubs encourage secondhand living. . . .

The Bible makes it clear that every time there is a story of faith, it is completely original. God's creative genius is endless. . . . Each life is a fresh canvas on which he uses lines and colors, shades and lights, textures and proportions that he has never used before.

RUN WITH THE HORSES

WORSHIP WITH JOY

When they said, "Let's go to the
house of GOD," my heart leaped for joy.

PSALM 122:1, THE MESSAGE

E ven in a time when church attendance is not considered to be on the upswing in the United States, the numbers are impressive. There are more people at worship on any given Sunday, for instance, than are at all the football games or on the golf links or fishing or taking walks in the woods. Worship is the single most popular act in this land.

So when we hear the psalmist say, "When they said, 'Let's go to the house of GOD,' my heart leaped for joy," we are not listening to the phony enthusiasm of a propagandist drumming up business for worship; we are witnessing what is typical of most Christians in most places at most times.

A LONG OBEDIENCE

BEAUTY IN THE WILDERNESS

When I was desperate, I called out, and
GOD got me out of a tight spot.

PSALM 34:6, THE MESSAGE

Everything is gong along fine: we've gotten a job, decorated the house, signed up for car payments. And then suddenly there's a radical change in our bodies, or our emotions, or our thinking, or our friends, or our job. We're out of control. We're in the wilderness.

This circumstantial wilderness is a terrible, frightening, and dangerous place; but I also believe it's a place of beauty. There are things to be seen, heard, and experienced in this wilderness that can be seen, heard, and experienced nowhere else. . . . We're plunged into an awareness of danger and death; at the very same moment we're plunged, if we let ourselves be, into an awareness of the great mystery of God.

LEAP OVER A WALL

LIVE FREELY

Live carefree before God; he is most careful with you.

1 PETER 5:7, THE MESSAGE

The personal dimension of the gospel is good news about ourselves. . . . No matter how well we manage to provide an appearance of competence and happiness, if we are filled with anxieties and guilt and hopelessness, we cannot make it. . . .

God's love and our salvation are completely expressed and fully accomplished in Jesus Christ. That is good news. As we receive him, we live freely and not apprehensively. We live in open praise and not in piggish greed. Our lives are changed from being obsessed with guilt and ridden with fear to being spontaneous and filled with hope. That's good news!

TRAVELING LIGHT

THE PRACTICE OF PRAYER

It was Sunday and I was in the Spirit, praying.

REVELATION 1:10, THE MESSAGE

After a few introductory sentences in the Revelation, we come upon St. John in the place and practice of prayer (1:9–10). . . .

At the end of the book he is still praying: "Amen. Come, Lord Jesus!" (22:20). St. John listens to God, is silent before God, sings to God, asks questions of God. . . .

St. John doesn't miss much. He reads and assimilates the Scriptures; he reads and feels the impact of the daily news. But neither ancient Scripture nor current event is left the way it arrives on his doorstep; it is all turned into prayer.

THE CONTEMPLATIVE PASTOR

GRACE AND LOVE

The foundations of the City walls were garnished with every precious gem imaginable. . . . The twelve gates were twelve pearls, each gate a single pear.

REVELATION 21:19, 21, THE MESSAGE

S t. John gives us a vision of heaven, for if we have no vision of heaven, we will almost certainly be leveled to a monochrome existence—colorless do-gooders who see everything in terms of black and white, whose lives are drab with moral drudgery. But the life of grace and the love of Christ are nothing if not extravagant. . . .

The light of heaven is not a blur of a forty-watt bulb, hanging naked in the night. It is *colors,* light that reveals the specific hue and texture of everything in creation. In the light we are surrounded by and washed in an exuberant Niagara of color.

REVERSED THUNDER

THE LIVING CENTER

Know this: GOD is God. . . .
We're his people, his well-tended sheep.

PSALM 100:2, THE MESSAGE

God is the living center of everything we are and everything we do. He is before, behind, over, beneath everything. If we separate any part of our lives from him, we are left holding an empty bag. Nothing can stand on its own as a good, apart from God. Anything wrenched from its context in God's creation and God's salvation is without substance. It is either God or nothing. No idea, no feeling, no truth, no pleasure can exist on its own.

FIVE SMOOTH STONES

SURPRISING VICTORIES

It is God who is at work in you, enabling you both
to will and to work for his good pleasure.

PHILIPPIANS 2:13, NRSV

In Jonah's escapist disobedience the sailors in the ship prayed to the Lord and entered into a life of faith (Jon. 1:16). . . . In Jonah's angry obedience, the Ninevites were all saved (Jon. 3:10).

God works his purposes through who we actually are, our rash disobedience and our heartless obedience, and generously uses our lives as he finds us to do his work.

He does it in such a way that it is almost impossible for us to take credit for any of it, but also in such a way that somewhere along the way we gasp in surprised pleasure at the victories he accomplishes.

UNDER THE UNPREDICTABLE PLANT

GOD'S GRAND IDEAS

"I have put my words in your mouth. . . .
I have set you this day over nations."

JEREMIAH 1:9–10, RSV

There is an enormous gap between what we think we can do and what God calls us to do. Our ideas of what we can do or want to do are trivial; God's ideas for us are grand.

It is not our feelings that determine our level of participation in life, nor our experience that qualifies us for what we will do and be. It is what God decides about us. God does not send us into the dangerous and exacting life of faith because we are qualified; he chooses us in order to qualify us for what he wants us to be and to do.

RUN WITH THE HORSES

THE CROSS—THE CENTER

*I am going to boast about nothing
but the Cross of our Master, Jesus Christ.*

GALATIANS 6:14, THE MESSAGE

The single, overwhelming fact of history is the crucifixion of Jesus Christ. There is no military battle, no geographical exploration, no scientific discovery, no literary creation, no artistic achievement, no moral heroism that compares with it. It is unique, massive, monumental, unprecedented, and unparalleled. The cross of Christ is not a small secret that may or may not get out. The cross of Christ is not a minor incident in the political history of the first century that is a nice illustration of courage. It is the center.

The cross of Christ is the central fact to which all other facts are subordinate.

TRAVELING LIGHT

GOD'S WILL

Blessed be GOD, my mountain. . . .
He's the bedrock on which I stand.

PSALM 144:1, THE MESSAGE

I don't know one thing about the future. I don't know what the next hour will hold. There may be sickness, accident, personal or world catastrophe. Before this day is over I may have to deal with death, pain, loss, rejection. I don't know what the future holds for me, for those I love, for my nation, for this world. Still, despite my ignorance and surrounded by tinny optimists and cowardly pessimists, I say that God will accomplish his will, and I cheerfully persist in living in the hope that nothing will separate me from Christ's love.

A LONG OBEDIENCE

SINGING AN OLD SONG

*I will meditate on all thy work,
and muse on thy mighty deeds.*

PSALM 77:12, RSV

Any place is the right place to begin to pray. But we must not be afraid of ending up some place quite different from where we start. The psalmist began by feeling sorry for himself and asking questions that seethed with insolence. He ended up singing an old song proclaiming might and grace.

The tiresome "I think of God, and I moan" in the course of prayer becomes the exhilarating "I will meditate on all thy work, and muse on thy mighty deeds."

WHERE YOUR TREASURE IS

LEAVE IT WITH GOD

Live generously and graciously
toward others, the way God lives toward you.

MATTHEW 5:48, THE MESSAGE

Saul made life difficult for David, but he didn't destroy him. If David had allowed Saul's hate to determine his life, he would have been destroyed. He maybe wouldn't have been killed, but he certainly would have been damned—reduced, cramped, and constricted by vengeance. When he was being chased down by Saul, he prayed his distress and anger and left it with God, Saul's sufficient judge. Saul's hate, instead of narrowing David and reducing him, in fact provided conditions in which he became large, expansive, and generous.

LEAP OVER A WALL

PLACE OF PRAYER

I've already run for
dear life straight to the arms of GOD.

PSALM 11:1, THE MESSAGE

David's life is the most exuberant life story in all the scriptures, maybe the most exuberant in all world history. It is also the most extensively narrated story in our Bible. We know more about David than any other person in the biblical communities of faith. . . .

The person in scripture who has the most extensively told story is the same person who is shown to be most at prayer. . . . He was a shepherd, guerrilla fighter, court musician, and politician. His entire life was lived in a sacred ordinary that we are apt, mistakenly, to call the secular. The regular place of prayer is the ordinary life.

ANSWERING GOD

GRACIOUS FORGIVENESS

Jesus' priesthood is permanent. He's there
from now to eternity to save everyone who comes
to God through him.

HEBREWS 7:24–25, THE MESSAGE

The Son of Man is a priest. A priest is a bridge. A priest presents God to us, he also presents us to God. He brings together the divine and the human. A priest mediates. He is just as much on God's side as on our side.

If we aspire after more than we are, a priest promises help. If we regret the mess we are in, a priest promises help. If the Son of Man does the work of priest, there is much to be in awe of but nothing to be afraid of: mediation results in loving union. If the Son of Man does the work of priest, there is much to be repented of but nothing of which to despair: mediation results in gracious forgiveness.

REVERSED THUNDER

PRAYERFUL AGENTS

Seek first the kingdom of God and His righteousness,
and all these things shall be added to you.

MATTHEW 6:33, NKJV

I n honor of His own Son whose death made possible the full invasion of divine power into the impossibilities of earth, God will do nothing apart from the prayers of the people His Son redeemed. The power is His; the privilege is ours.

We who are in Christ have no reason to fear or surrender to hell's program. We have been redeemed to be prayerful agents of God's blessing, authority, and power on earth; to pray for the earthly manifestation of His heavenly righteousness and will.

That will happen when we seek God's kingdom first.

LIKE DEW YOUR YOUTH

WE TAKE GOD SERIOUSLY

If GOD doesn't guard the city,
the night watchman might as well nap.

PSALM 127:1, THE MESSAGE

The main difference between Christians and others is that we take God seriously and they do not.

We really do believe that he is the central reality of all existence.

We really do pay attention to what he is and what he does.

We really do order our lives in response to that reality and not to some other.

A LONG OBEDIENCE

COMMITMENT IN FAITH

*There has never been the slightest doubt in my mind
that the God who started this great work in you
would keep at it and bring it to a flourishing finish.*

PHILIPPIANS 1:6, THE MESSAGE

The function of religion is not to make people feel good but to make them good. Love? Yes, God loves us. But his love is passionate and seeks faithful, committed love in return. God does not want tame pets to fondle and feed; he wants mature, free people who will respond to him in authentic individuality. For that to happen there must be honesty and truth. The self must be toppled from its pedestal. There must be pure hearts and clear intelligence, confession of sin and commitment in faith.

RUN WITH THE HORSES

RESPONDING TO GOD

By an act of faith, Abraham said yes to God's call.

HEBREWS 11:8, THE MESSAGE

Somewhere in the shadows of the nineteenth century B. C., . . . Abraham heard God's call, left home and began a long trek westward. He left his religion, his home, his culture, and his security. God was more important to Abraham than anything else—country, comfort, culture. . . .

God offers himself in a personal relationship with us; we respond with nothing less than our lives. Everything in and about us—our work, our families, our affections, our plans, our memories, our play, our possessions—is coordinated and arranged in that foundational, responding, living relationship with God.

TRAVELING LIGHT

EMPTIED AND FILLED

Christ Jesus . . . emptied himself, taking the form
of a slave, being born in human likeness.

PHILIPPIANS 2:5–7, NRSV

St. Paul's description of Jesus, "emptied himself," is often cited as the center point in the work of Incarnation, the making of our salvation.

Emptying is prelude to filling. The Son of God empties himself of prerogative, of divine rights, of status and reputation, on order to be the one whom God uses to fill up creation and creatures with the glory of salvation. A bucket, no matter what wonderful things it contains, is of no use for the next task at hand until it is emptied.

THE CONTEMPLATIVE PASTOR

OUR BELIEFS

The fool says in his heart, "There is no God."

PSALM 14:1, RSV

G. K. Chesterton once said that if he were a landlord what he would most want to know about his tenants was not their employment, nor their income, but their beliefs, if there was any way he could truly find out. For it would be their beliefs that would determine their honesty, their relationships, and their stewardship of the property. An adequate income is no proof against dishonesty. A reputable job is no guarantee against profligacy. Our beliefs are not off-the-cuff answers we give to an opinion survey; our beliefs are the deepest things about us.

WHERE YOUR TREASURE IS

WE LIVE IN HOPE

I have it all planned out—
plans to take care of you, not abandon you,
plans to give you the future you hope for.

JEREMIAH 29:11, THE MESSAGE

Hope acts on the conviction that God will complete the work he has begun even when the appearances, especially when the appearances, oppose it.

Every person we meet must be drawn into that expectation. Every situation in which we find ourselves must be included in the kingdom that we are convinced God is bringing into being. Hope is buying into what we believe. . . .

It is, of course, far easier to languish in despair than to live in hope, for when we live in despair we don't have to do anything or risk anything. If we live in hope, we go against the stream.

RUN WITH THE HORSES

ENDLESS POSSIBILITIES

You are Christ's body—that's who you are!
You must never forget this.

1 CORINTHIANS 12:27, THE MESSAGE

Important in any community of faith is an ever-renewed expectation in what God is doing with our brothers and sisters in the faith. . . . We refuse to predict our brother's behavior, our sister's growth. Each person in the community is unique; each is specially loved and particularly led by the Spirit of God.

A community of faith flourishes when we view each other with this expectancy, wondering what God will do today in this one, in that one. . . . They are new persons each morning, endless in their possibilities.

A LONG OBEDIENCE

A SENSE OF MUTUALITY

Let the peace of Christ keep you in tune with each other, in step with each other.

COLOSSIANS 3:15, THE MESSAGE

E ach of us has strengths to share with another and knowledge with which to guide another. But that does not make us self-sufficient. . . .

Sometimes we are the friend who steps in to help; sometimes we are the friend who is helped. In either case our experience of freedom is deepened. We are no longer imprisoned in our strengths; we are no longer paralyzed by our needs. We acquire a sense of mutuality as we help and are helped.

TRAVELING LIGHT

GOD SAVES FROM SIN

"If your sins are blood-red, they'll be snow-white."

ISAIAH 1:18, THE MESSAGE

"I have sinned against the LORD" (2 Sam.12:13, RSV) is a sentence full of hope. It's full of hope because it's a sentence full of God.

The Latin phrase *felix culpa,* usually attributed to Augustine, puts the hope in a slogan: "O happy sin!" Only when I recognize and confess my sin am I in a position to recognize and respond to the God who saves me from my sin. If I'm ignorant of or indifferent to my sin, I'm ignorant of or indifferent to the great and central good news: "Jesus saves!"

LEAP OVER A WALL

FIRST STEPS

GOD, listen! Listen to my prayer,
listen to the pain in my cries.

PSALM 102:1, THE MESSAGE

Human hurt is not a very promising first step to the accomplishment of wholeness. Human hate is not a very promising first step to the establishment of righteousness. Nevertheless, when prayed, they are steps, first steps into the presence of God where we learn that he has ways of dealing with what we bring him that are both other and better than what we had in mind. But until we are in prayer, we are not teachable. It is better to pray badly than not to pray at all.

ANSWERING GOD

THE GREAT "NO"

The other disciple, . . . went into the tomb,
took one look at the evidence, and believed.

JOHN 20:8, THE MESSAGE

The empty tomb, a story that the canonical Gospels agree is essential for understanding the resurrection, is the experience of a great "no." It represents what humanity does not have to, in fact, cannot, do. I don't have to take care of God; he can take care of himself. I don't have to watch over his body; I don't have to protect him from his enemies; I don't have to manage him, defend him, or tell him what needs to be done next.

The tomb is empty—which means that I can go home and go about the work to which I have been called and commanded.

FIVE SMOOTH STONES

WARMTH AND SUNLIGHT

His face was like the sun shining in full strength.

REVELATION 1:16, RSV

When Moses returned from the mountain of revelation, his face was shining so brightly that the people could not look on it. The Aaronic benediction prays, "The LORD make his face to shine upon you, and be gracious to you" (Num. 6:25, RSV). In Christ the blessing of God is made personal in the shining face: "His face was like the sun shining in full strength." God in Christ is warmth and sunlight.

REVERSED THUNDER

WORK DONE WELL

Go to work in the morning and
stick to it until evening without watching the clock.

ECCLESIASTES 11:6, THE MESSAGE

Any work done faithfully and well is difficult. It is no harder for me to do my job well than for any other person, and no less. There are no easy tasks in the Christian way; there are only tasks that can be done faithfully or erratically, with joy or with resentment.

A LONG OBEDIENCE

SHOUT IN APPLAUSE

Write to the . . . church . . . the words
of the Amen, the faithful and true witness.

REVELATION 3:14, NRSV

Justin Martyr in his description of Christian worship in the middle of the second century (c. 150 A. D.), tells us that prayers always concluded with a vigorous amen by the congregation. Justin uses a colorful and enthusiastic word to describe their amen—*epeuphemei,* "shout in applause." The word expressed the conviction that not only would prayers be fulfilled by God in the future, but that the fulfillment was already present in Christ. . . .

When we Christians say or sing or shout, "amen," God hears our unequivocating assent to his irrevocable Yes to us—the Yes of our redeemer Lamb, the Yes of our creator King.

REVERSED THUNDER

MAY

God is making
a people for his glory.

SPOKEN AND WRITTEN

*The Word became flesh and
lived among us, and we have seen his glory.*

JOHN 1:14, NRSV

The Christian believes that God speaks and that, as a result of that speaking, all things are brought into being: nature and super-nature, the stuff of creation and the relationships of the covenant, and, eventually, scripture. God's word brings the cosmos into existence. God's word accomplishes forgiveness. "For he spoke, and it came to be" (Ps. 33:9, NRSV). God has the first word, he has the last word, and all the words in between are spoken in a vocabulary and by means of a grammar that are his gifts to us. . . .

The word of God was spoken before it was written. Jesus was seen and touched and heard, before he was written about.

REVERSED THUNDER

GOD'S RULE

When everything and everyone is finally
under God's rule, the Son will step down, taking
his place with everyone else, showing that God's rule
is absolutely comprehensive—a perfect ending!

1 CORINTHIANS 15:28, THE MESSAGE

What is God doing? He is saving; he is rescuing; he is blessing; he is providing; he is judging; he is healing; he is enlightening. There is a spiritual war in progress, an all-out moral battle. There is evil and cruelty, unhappiness and illness. There is superstition and ignorance, brutality and pain. God is in continuous and energetic battle against all of it.

God is for life and against death. God is for love and against hate. God is for hope and against despair. God is for heaven and against hell. There is no neutral ground in the universe. Every square foot of space is contested.

RUN WITH THE HORSES

OVERFLOWING JOY

Those who went off with heavy hearts will come home laughing, with armloads of blessings.

PSALM 126:6, THE MESSAGE

Christian joy is not an escape from sorrow. Pain and hardship still come, but they are unable to drive out the happiness of the redeemed.

Joy is what God gives, not what we work up. Laughter is the delight that things are working together for good to them that love God, not the giggles that betray the nervousness of a precarious defense system. The joy that develops in the Christian way of discipleship is an overflow of spirits that comes from feeling good not about yourself but about God. We find that his ways are dependable, his promises sure.

A LONG OBEDIENCE

WE NEED GOD

I pray to GOD—my life a prayer
—and wait for what he'll say and do.

PSALM 130:5, THE MESSAGE

There isn't a single area of our lives in which we're self-sufficient. We need God. We never develop or graduate to a state in which we don't need God. I once heard Isaac Bashevis Singer, master storyteller in Yiddish, say in a radio interview, "I pray only when I am in trouble; but I am in trouble all the time so I pray all the time."

Everywhere throughout the biblical revelation we're encouraged to come to God with our lists of requests. God is generous and never runs out of blessings. God delights in giving—it's what he does best.

LEAP OVER A WALL

SET FREE

*"If you stick with this, living out
what I tell you, . . . the truth will free you."*

JOHN 8:31–32, THE MESSAGE

Every Christian story is a freedom story. Each tells how a person has been set free from the confines of small ideas, from the chains of what other people think, from the emotional cages of guilt and regret, from the prisons of the self, sin-separated from God. We are free to change. The process of that change is always a good story, but it is never a neat formula.

We would prefer a formula. But freedom doesn't come by formula. It is a story that is worked out within all the complexities and ambiguities of the self and of history.

TRAVELING LIGHT

LISTENING TO OTHERS

Reach out to those who are oppressed.
Share their burdens. . . .

GALATIANS 6:2, THE MESSAGE

Listening is in short supply in the world today; people aren't used to being listened to. I know how easy it is to avoid the tough, intense work of listening by being busy—as when I let a hospital patient know there are ten more people I have to see. . . .

Speaking to people does not have the same personal intensity as listening to them. The question I put to myself is not "How many people have you spoken to about Christ this week?" but "How many people have you listened to in Christ this week?" . . .

I can't listen if I'm busy.

THE CONTEMPLATIVE PASTOR

THE WORD WE HEAR

*I'm thanking you, GOD, out in the
streets, singing your praises in town and country.*

PSALM 108:3, THE MESSAGE

The psalmists are not interested in human potential; they are passionate about *God*— the obedience shaping, will-transforming, sin-revoking, praise-releasing God.

The Psalms come from a people who hear God speak to them and realize that it is the most important word they will ever hear spoken. They decide to respond. They answer. The word they hear from God takes precedence over every human word: human wisdom, human advice, human discourses, human inquiry.

ANSWERING GOD

THE ORDINARY CHURCH

May God, who puts all things together, . . .
provide you with everything you need to please him.

HEBREWS 13:20–21, THE MESSAGE

Ordinary congregations are God's choice for the form the church takes. . . . Of all the ways in which to engage the enterprise of church, this has to be the most absurd—this haphazard collection of people who somehow get assembled into pews on Sundays, half-heartedly sing a few songs most of them don't like, tune in and out of a sermon according to the state of their digestion and the preacher's decibels. . . .

But the people in these pews are also people who suffer deeply and find God in their suffering. These are men and women who make love commitments, are faithful to them through trial and temptation, and bear spirit-fruits that bless the people around them.

UNDER THE UNPREDICTABLE PLANT

GOD CALLS US

God shows his love for us in that
while we were yet sinners Christ died for us.

ROMANS 5:8, RSV

E laborate arguments about the power of God and the love of God, even if they are stated with the most forceful logic, never seem to be the key to initiating a person into the actual experience of trusting God. What we do see happen is that people trust God when they experience in a personal way God's treatment of them. They find that even though they are unacceptable, God through Christ accepts them.

God calls us; we answer. God forgives us; we accept His forgiveness. God acts toward us in a way that draws forth our trust; and we trust Him.

LIKE DEW YOUR YOUTH

NOT MY WILL

"Father, if it is Your will, take this cup away from Me;
nevertheless not My will, but Yours, be done."

LUKE 22:42, NKJV

Insistent encouragement is given by many voices today for living a better life. I welcome the encouragement. But the counsel that accompanies the encouragement has introduced no end of mischief in our society, and I am in strenuous opposition to it. The counsel is that we can arrive at our full humanness by gratifying our desires. It has been a recipe for misery for millions.

The biblical counsel in these matters is clear: "Not My will, but Yours be done."

RUN WITH THE HORSES

A WELL-PLACED "NO"

Run for dear life from evil;
hold on for dear life to good.

ROMANS 12:9, THE MESSAGE

Our capacity to say "no," is one of the most impressive features of our language. The negative is our access to freedom. Only humans can say "no." Animals can't say "no." Animals do what instinct dictates. The judicious, well-placed "no" frees us from many a blind alley, many a rough detour, frees us from debilitating distractions and seductive sacrilege. The art of saying "no" sets us free to follow Jesus.

Following Jesus means *not* following your impulses and appetites and whims and dreams, all of which are sufficiently damaged by sin to make them unreliable guides for getting anyplace worth going.

TRAVELING LIGHT

THE EDGE OF GLORY

Thank you for your love,
thank you for your faithfulness.

PSALM 138:2, THE MESSAGE

Why did David dance? David, dancing before the Ark, reckless and joyful.

David had been living dangerously all his life—with lions and bears, a taunting giant and a murderous king, marauding Philistines and cunning Amalekites, in wilderness caves and wadis. And with and in God: running and hiding, praying and loving. . . . In and under these conditions David had learned to live openly, daringly, trustingly, and exultantly before God.

In God, David had access to life that exceeded his capacity to measure or control. He was on the edge of mystery, of glory. And so he danced.

LEAP OVER A WALL

FACE THE FLAWS

Be angry but sin not.

EPHESIANS 4:26, RSV

"*Be angry.*" No day is perfect. Things go wrong. Some things always go wrong, many of them out of spite, malice, and blasphemy. Face squarely the worst of the day, and be angry. Don't make excuses for yourself or others. Don't paper over any flaws. You do well to be angry. "*But sin not.*" Your anger is not a work agenda for you to plan a vengeance that will fix the wrong. What is wrong with the world is God's business.

ANSWERING GOD

LIVING IN THE MIDDLE

"I am the Alpha and the Omega," says the Lord God, who is and who was and who is to come.

REVELATION 1:8, NRSV

We believe that God is at the beginning of all things, and we believe that God is at the conclusion of all life—in St. John's striking epigram: "the Alpha and the Omega" (Rev. 1:8). It is routine among us to assume that the beginning was good ("and God saw everything that he had made, and behold it was very good"). It is agreed among us that the conclusion will be good ("And I saw a new heaven and a new earth").

That would seem to guarantee that everything between the good beginning and the good ending will also be good. But it doesn't turn out that way. . . . I am rejected by a parent, . . . injured by another's carelessness. All of this in a life that at its creation was very good and at its conclusion will be completed according to God's design.

REVERSED THUNDER

THE MESS OF SIN

He forgives your sins—every one.

PSALM 103:3, THE MESSAGE

Forgiveness is not a midpoint between condoning and condemning. It is not a balance between something gentle and something harsh. It is not an apothecary's mixture of two parts acceptance and one part punishment. It is something entirely different. It is what God has shown us as His way of dealing with . . . sin.

The only way to understand forgiveness is to understand it as what God does for us through Jesus Christ. Forgiveness is not a human act; it is not what we do to repair the damage our sins have caused. It is a divine act. It is what God does to deal with the mess of our sins. Insofar as we can engage in it at all it is as participants in what God is doing in Jesus Christ.

LIKE DEW YOUR YOUTH

GOD WORKS IN JESUS

Put God in charge of your work,
then what you've planned will take place.

PROVERBS 16:3, THE MESSAGE

We live in a universe and in a history where God is working before anything else. Work is an activity of God.

The work of God is defined and described in the pages of Scripture. We have models of creation, acts of redemption, examples of help and compassion, paradigms of comfort and salvation. One of the reasons that Christians read Scripture repeatedly and carefully is to find out just how God works in Jesus Christ so that we can work in the name of Jesus Christ.

A LONG OBEDIENCE

A PEOPLE OF GOD

We're the clay and you're our potter:
all of us are what you made us.

ISAIAH 64:8, THE MESSAGE

God is at work making a people for his glory. A people of God. Persons created in the image of God. . . .

Each human being is an inseparable union of necessity and freedom. There is no human being who is not useful with a part to play in what God is doing. And there is no human being who is not unique with special lines and colors and forms distinct from anyone else.

God shapes us for his eternal purposes and he begins right here. The dust out which we are made and the image of God into which we are made are one and the same.

RUN WITH THE HORSES

LIVING BY FAITH

When everything was hopeless,
Abraham believed anyway.

ROMANS 4:18, THE MESSAGE

Can you find any arrows painted in that wilderness into which Abraham ventured? Did he have a rule book that showed him step by step what he must do to please God? . . . No, he lived by faith. . . .

Did Abraham have a twenty-year plan with carefully defined objectives as he launched his important career as father of the faithful? No, there were delays, interruptions, detours, failures. He didn't do it all correctly—he didn't live without doubt or sin or despair—but he did it. He followed and confessed and prayed and believed. God was alive for him. God was the center for him.

TRAVELING LIGHT

DESCRIBING GRACE

I do not cease to give thanks for you,
 remembering you in my prayers.

EPHESIANS 1:16, RSV

Writing to the Ephesians, Paul says: "For this reason, because I have heard of your faith in the Lord Jesus and your love toward all the saints, I do not cease to give thanks for you, remembering you in my prayers" (Eph. 1:15–16, RSV). Assuming that the Ephesian church had the same percentage of sinners in it as modern ones do (namely, 100 percent), it would be a mistake to envy Paul his congregation, a congregation that it was possible to address so gratefully. It is better to admire Paul's ability to see God's action in those people. . . . His passion was for describing grace.

THE CONTEMPLATIVE PASTOR

TO LOVE IS TO GROW

Out of respect for Christ,
be courteously reverent to one another.

EPHESIANS 5:21, THE MESSAGE

L ove launches us into new territory. To explore the new, the old must be left. It means leaving earlier levels of accomplishment and relationship and growing into new ones. Every act of love is a risk of the self. There are no guarantees in love. Much can go wrong: we can get hurt; we can be rejected; we can be deceived. But without risking these perils there can only be a repetition of old patterns, the routine of old comfort.

The self cannot be itself if it does not grow, and for a creature made in the image of God to grow is to love.

WHERE YOUR TREASURE IS

MORE ALIVE

Take on an entirely new way of life
—a God-fashioned life. . . .

EPHESIANS 4:24, THE MESSAGE

Pliny the Elder once said that the Romans, when they couldn't make a building beautiful, made it big. The practice continues to be popular: If we can't do it well, we make it larger. We add dollars to our income, rooms to our houses, activities to our schedules, appointments to our calendars. And the quality of life diminishes with each addition.

On the other hand, every time we retrieve a part of our life from the crowd and respond to God's call to us, we are that much more ourselves, more human. Every time we reject the habits of the crowd and practice the disciplines of faith, we become a little more alive.

RUN WITH THE HORSES

IN GOD'S IMAGE

Teach me how to live to please you,
because you're my God.

PSALM 143:8, THE MESSAGE

Our lives are lived well only when they are lived on the terms of their creation, with God loving and us being loved, with God making and us being made, with God revealing and us understanding, with God commanding and us responding.

Being a Christian means accepting the terms of creation, accepting God as our maker and redeemer, and growing day by day into an increasingly glorious creature in Christ, developing joy, experiencing the marvel of being made in the image of God.

A Long Obedience

AN OPEN APPROACH

For you who revere my name the sun
of righteousness shall rise, with healing in its wings.

MALACHI 4:2, NRSV

In the Christian life our primary task isn't to avoid sin, which is impossible anyway, but to *recognize* sin. The fact is that we're sinners. But there's an enormous amount of self-deception in sin. When this is combined with devil-deception, the task of recognition is compounded. . . .

Our approach to sin, then, is characterized not by warnings and threats but by encouragements to honesty, invitations to come out in the open and greet the "sun of righteousness" who rises "with healing in its wings."

LEAP OVER A WALL

HONEST IN OUR HURTS

*Pile your troubles on GOD's shoulders
—he'll carry your load, he'll help you out.*

PSALM 55:22, THE MESSAGE

It is easy to be honest before God with our hallelujahs; it is somewhat more difficult to be honest in our hurts; it is nearly impossible to be honest before God in the dark emotions of our hate. So we commonly suppress our negative emotions. . . . But when we pray the psalms, these classic prayers of God's people, we find that will not do. We must pray who we actually are, not who we think we are, not who we think we should be.

In prayer, all is not sweetness and light. The way of prayer is not to cover our unlovely emotions so that they will appear respectable, but expose them so that they can be enlisted in the work of the kingdom.

ANSWERING GOD

GOD IS LIGHT

The light shines in the darkness,
and the darkness has not overcome it.

JOHN 1:5, RSV

No one seems completely at home in the dark, even though most of us learn to accustom ourselves to it. We invent devices to make the dark less threatening—a candle, a fire, a flashlight, a lamp. In the darkness we are liable to lose perspective and proportion: nightmares terrorize us, fears paralyze us.

A light that shines in the darkness shows that the terror and the chaos have no objective reality to them. . . . If there is something to be feared, the light shows the evil in proportionate relationship to all that is not to be feared.

We do not live in darkness, but in light. God is light.

REVERSED THUNDER

LIVING BY FAITH

Round the throne were twenty-four thrones, and
seated on the thrones were twenty-four elders clad in
white garments, with golden crowns upon their heads.

REVELATION 4:4, RSV

T he twenty-four elders are a double twelve, the
twelve Hebrew tribes and the twelve Christian
apostles, the old Israel and the new Church.

The throne assembles around itself that which
has been directed godward through centuries of
living by faith: the sacrifice and obedience, the
preaching and praising, the repenting and offering
of the people of Israel named after Jacob's sons, and
along with them the twelve apostles sent forth by
Jesus in acts of healing and blessing, feeding and
helping, delivering and preaching. All are gathered
around their center.

REVERSED THUNDER

APPEALS TO PRIDE

*The purity of human hearts is
tested by giving them a little fame.*

PROVERBS 27:21, THE MESSAGE

Our ancestors believed that humility was the human spirit tempered and resilient and strong. They knew that it was difficult. They knew that even those who admired and professed it were highly prone to subverting it in practice.

But in America even the pretense to humility has been abandoned. We are led off to assertiveness-training workshops and enrolled in management-by-objectives seminars. We are bombarded with techniques by which we are promised to be able to make an impact on society. Nearly all of them turn out to be appeals, in ways subtle or crass, to pride.

WHERE YOUR TREASURE IS

DETERMINED DELIVERANCE

*God so loved the world that
he gave his only Son, that whoever believes in him
should not perish but have eternal life.*

JOHN 3:16, RSV

The root meaning in Hebrew of "salvation" is to be broad, to become spacious, to enlarge. It carries the sense of deliverance from an existence that has become compressed, confined, and cramped.

Salvation is the plot of history. It is the most comprehensive theme of Scripture, overtaking and surpassing catastrophe. Salvation is God's determination to rescue his creation; it is his activity in recovering the world. It is personal and impersonal, it deals with souls and cities, it touches sin and sickness. . . . There are no fine distinctions about who or what or when—the whole lost world is invaded, infiltrated, beckoned, invited, wooed.

REVERSED THUNDER

WHEN GOD SPEAKS

"The LORD says . . . the LORD has sworn."

PSALM 110:1, 4, RSV

Psalm 110 established its eminence in the early Christians' community by centering the self in the God who speaks. They knew they were in a messed-up world and that something had to be done about it. They also knew their good works and good intentions were flawed in such a way that they only made it worse. . . .

How were they to do it? They prayed Psalm 110. It shaped their understanding of who they were and their place in the world by what it declared that world to be: when God speaks things happen.

WHERE YOUR TREASURE IS

NOT BY WORKS

A man is not justified by works
of the law but through faith in Jesus Christ.

GALATIANS 2:16, RSV

In some ways Christians are the least religious people in town—there is so much that we don't believe! We don't believe in good-luck charms, in horoscopes, in fate. We don't believe the world's promises or the world's curses. And we don't believe—this comes to some as a surprise!—in good works.

Paul repeats the phrase "not by works of the law" three times in two verses. He means something quite specific by it. He means the acts that we perform in order to get God's approval. He means religious or moral activity that is designed to save our own skin. It is good behavior or religious behavior that is performed because someone else is looking, or because God is looking.

TRAVELING LIGHT

SILENCE IS ESSENTIAL

You're my place of quiet retreat;
I wait for your Word to renew me.

PSALM 119:114, THE MESSAGE

Silence in prayer is not the absence of sound that occurs when we run out of things to say. It is not the embarrassing speechlessness that results from shyness. It is something positive, something fertile. It is being more interested in what God will say to me than in getting out my speech to him. It is a preference for hearing God's word over saying my word. . . .

Talk in prayer is essential but it is also partial. Silence is also essential.

WHERE YOUR TREASURE IS

It's always God
with whom
we have to do.

HOLY PLANS

Before I shaped you in the womb, I knew
all about you. Before you saw the light of day,
I had holy plans for you.

JEREMIAH 1:5, THE MESSAGE

We are curious about God. We make inquiries about God. We read books about God. We get into late night bull sessions about God. We drop into church from time to time to see what is going on with God. We indulge in an occasional sunset or symphony to cultivate a feeling of reverence for God.

But that is not the reality of our lives with God. . . . Long before we got interested in the subject of God, before it ever crossed our minds that God might be important, He singled us out as important. Before we were formed in the womb, God knew us.

RUN WITH THE HORSES

A LONG OBEDIENCE

I've got my eye on the goal,
where God is beckoning us onward—to Jesus.

PHILIPPIANS 3:14, THE MESSAGE

Everyone is in a hurry. The persons whom I lead in worship, among whom I counsel, visit, pray, preach and teach, want shortcuts. They want me to help them fill out the form that will get them instant credit (in eternity). They are impatient for results.

But the Christian life cannot mature under such conditions. . . . Freidrich Nietzche, who saw this era of spiritual truth with great clarity, wrote, "The essential thing 'in heaven and earth' is . . . that there should be long obedience in the same direction."

A LONG OBEDIENCE

THE LORD REIGNS

The LORD reigns; he is robed in majesty.

PSALM 93:1, RSV

Whether men and women know it or not they are now living under God's rule. Some live in rebellion that can be either defiant or ignorant. Some live in an obedience that can be either reluctant or devout. But no one lives apart from it. . . .

There are no days when the rule is not in operation. The week is not divided into one Lord's day when the rule of God is acknowledged and six human days in which factories, stock exchange, legislatures, media personalities, and military juntas take charge and rule.

Neither ignorance nor indifference diminishes God's rule. Day after day "the LORD reigns."

WHERE YOUR TREASURE IS

PARTICIPATING IN GOD'S WORK

Hard work always pays off.

PROVERBS 14:23, THE MESSAGE

I n the beginning, God went to work. A six-day work-week concluding in worship frames the entire spirituality of creation, with God in the role of worker (Gen 1:1–2:4). In the second creation story, man and woman are placed in the garden as workers, employed at tasks assigned by their maker (Gen. 2).

Work is the primary context for our spirituality. Most children's play is practice for adult work. We play our way into adult work; our games are apprenticeships. The spiritual life begins—seriously begins—when we get a job and go to work.

Work is our Spirit-anointed participation in God's work.

LEAP OVER A WALL

MADE WHOLE

*"He who had set me apart before I
was born, and had called me through his grace,
was pleased to reveal his Son to me."*

GALATIANS 1:15–16, RSV

God revealed himself in the person of Jesus to Paul. It was as if God said, "Listen, Paul, you have it all wrong. You have good ideas, your theology is intelligent enough, your sincerity is above reproach, but you have it all wrong. You think religion is a matter of knowing things and doing things. It is not. It is a matter of letting God do something for you—letting him love you, letting him save you, letting him bless you, letting him command you. Your part is to look and believe, to pray and obey. For a start I am going to show myself to you in Jesus. In him you will see that what concerns me is being with you, making you whole."

TRAVELING LIGHT

TRUSTING GOD

We love, because he first loved us.

1 JOHN 4:19, RSV

In matters that are at the very core of our existence, we learn through demonstration, by having truth done to and for us. God demonstrated in Jesus Christ. He did it first, to make it possible for us to do it. "We love, because he first loved us" is the way Saint John put it.

Christians learn to trust God not because they have been convinced by arguments that they should trust Him but because they have been treated by God in a loving, accepting, trusting way *before* they were lovable, acceptable, or trustworthy.

LIKE DEW YOUR YOUTH

AN ACT OF OBEDIENCE

GOD is great, and worth a thousand Hallelujahs.

PSALM 96:4, THE MESSAGE

We think that if we don't *feel* something there can be no authenticity in *doing* it. But the wisdom of God says something different: that we can act ourselves into a new way of feeling much quicker than we can *feel* ourselves into a new way of acting. Worship in an *act* that develops feelings for God, not a *feeling* for God that is expressed in an act of worship. When we obey the command to praise God in worship, our deep, essential need to be in relationship with God is nurtured.

A LONG OBEDIENCE

DARING TO LOVE

*If we love one another, God dwells deeply within us,
and his love becomes complete in us—perfect love!*

1 JOHN 4:12, THE MESSAGE

E very day I put love on the line. There is
nothing I am less good at than love. I am
better in competition than in love. I am far better
at responding to my instincts and ambitions to get
ahead and make my mark than I am at figuring
out how to love one another. I am schooled and
trained in acquisitive skills, in getting my own
way. And yet I decide, every day, to set aside what
I can do best and attempt what I do very clumsily—
open myself to the frustrations and failures of
loving, daring to believe that failing in love is
better than succeeding in pride.

A LONG OBEDIENCE

THE ANTIDOTE IS PRAYER

As a father pities his children,
so the LORD pities those who fear Him.

PSALM 103:13, NKJV

Self-pity almost always deals with accurate facts: that man does have a better car than I do; that woman does have more considerate husband than I do; that person does have a better digestive system than I do. . . .

The antidote is well known. . . . It is simply, prayer. The initial impulse to pray often comes from self-pity. We feel sorry for ourselves and because God is widely known to be pitying, we enlist him in feeling sorry for us. But it doesn't work that way. In prayer our self-pity meets up with a stronger, healthier energy and gets itself transformed.

WHERE YOUR TREASURE IS

GATHERED INTO GOD

*Commune with your own
hearts on your beds, and be silent.*

PSALM 4:4, RSV

"*Commune with your own hearts on your beds.*" Speak to yourself. Listen to yourself. In the crossfire of daytime voices, we become strangers to ourselves. Get acquainted again with the being that God created, not just the passport version that you have used to get more or less successfully through the day.

"*And be silent.*" Nothing more need be said. No explanations, no boasts, no apologies. This is who you are. There is something more important than liking or not liking yourself, more significant than the day's accomplishments and failures; there is *you*. In the silence, simply be the person that God is gathering into salvation.

ANSWERING GOD

DESTINED FOR GOD

In the beginning was the Word, and the
Word was with God, and the Word was God.

JOHN 1:1, NRSV

The Christian community needs theologians to keep us *thinking* about God and not just making random guesses.

At the deepest levels of our lives we require a God whom we can worship with our whole mind and heart and strength. The taste for eternity can never be bred out of us by a secularizing genetics. Our existence is derived from God and destined for God. St. John stands in the front ranks of the great company of theologians who convince by their disciplined and vigorous thinking that *theos* and *logos* belong together, that we live in a creation and not a madhouse.

REVERSED THUNDER

A WAY OF BLESSING

All you who fear GOD, how blessed you are!
How happily you walk on his smooth straight road!

PSALM 128:1, THE MESSAGE

The road we travel is the well-traveled road of discipleship. It is not the way of boredom or despair or confusion. It is not a miserable groping but a way of blessing.

There are no tricks involved in getting in on this life of blessing, and no luck required. We simply become Christians and begin the life of faith. We acknowledge God as our maker and lover and accept Christ as the means by which we can be in living relationship with God.

A LONG OBEDIENCE

A MARRIAGE

Love never gives up.
Love cares more for others than for self.

1 CORINTHIANS 13:4, THE MESSAGE

When I talk with people who come to me in preparation for marriage I often say, "Weddings are easy; marriages are difficult." The couple want to plan a wedding; I want to plan a marriage. They want to know where the bridesmaids will stand; I want to develop a plan for forgiveness. They want to discuss the music of the wedding; I want to talk about the emotions of the marriage.

I can do a wedding in twenty minutes with my eyes shut. A marriage takes year after year after year of alert, wide-eyed attention.

RUN WITH THE HORSES

DIVERSITY

He made the entire human race . . .
with plenty of time and space for living so we could
seek after God, and . . . actually find him.

ACTS 17:26, THE MESSAGE

The biblical story of creating makes it clear that the great variety in creation is not a matter of some things being better and other things being worse. The repeated refrain is "And God saw that is was good." The diversity is goodness abundantly expressed. . . .

We are free in relationship to each other, discovering an equal acceptance. Other persons are not enemies to fear, not superior beings to envy, not deadbeats to avoid. In Christ every person is or can be experienced in a new way, a person we are free to receive and love without fear of being diminished or intimidated.

TRAVELING LIGHT

MY REFUGE

O LORD my God, in thee do I take refuge.

PSALM 7:1, RSV

In David's prayers *refuge* refers to a good experience, but what got him to refuge was a bad experience. He started out running for his life; and at some point he found the life he was running for, and the name for that life was God. "God is my refuge."

This happens all the time. It's one of the fundamental surprises in spirituality. Whatever we start out feeling or doing or thinking can lead us to God, whether directly or meanderingly. . . . We rarely start with God. We start with the immediate data of our lives—a messy house, a balky car, a cranky spouse, a recalcitrant child. . . . We start out being desperate in the wilderness of En-gedi, and before we know it we're ecstatic in the wilderness of God.

WHERE YOUR TREASURE IS

FRUITS OF FAITH

He brings gifts into our lives, much the
same way that fruit appears in an orchard—
things like affection for others.

GALATIANS 5:22, THE MESSAGE

Fruits are not something made, manufactured or engineered. . . . They are the results of a life of faith created by God.

The person who lives a life of faith finds fruits appearing in unlikely places at unanticipated times. That is, we find that there is far more to our lives than we bring to them. Fruit is the appropriate metaphor. We do not produce it by our own effort. We do not purchase it from another. It is not a reward for doing good deeds, like a merit badge, a gold medal, a blue ribbon. Fruits are simply there. Sometimes we experience them in another, sometimes in ourselves.

TRAVELING LIGHT

THAT'S GOD'S BUSINESS

GOD, I'm not trying to rule the roost, . . .
I haven't meddled where I have no business.

PSALM 131:1, THE MESSAGE

I will not try to run my own life or the lives of others; that is God's business. I will not pretend to invent the meaning of the universe; I will accept what God has shown its meaning to be. I will not strut about demanding that I be treated as the center of my family or my neighborhood or my work, but seek to discover where I fit and do what I am good at. The soul, clamoring for attention and arrogantly parading it's importance, is calmed and quieted so that it can be itself, truly.

A LONG OBEDIENCE

"SIN"—A SPIRITUAL TERM

Scrub away my guilt,
soak out my sins in your laundry.

PSALM 51:2, THE MESSAGE

The basic, fundamental condition of our humanity is God. We're created by God. We're redeemed by God. We're blessed by God. We're provided for by God. We're loved by God. Sin is the denial or ignorance or avoidance of that basic condition. Sin is the word we use to designate the perverseness of will by which we attempt being our own gods, or making for ourselves other gods.

Sin isn't essentially a moral term, designating items of wrongdoing; it's a spiritual term, designating our God-avoidance and our god-pretensions. . . . The subtlety of sin is that it doesn't feel like sin when we're doing it; it feels godlike.

LEAP OVER A WALL

OUR GOOD CREATION

In the image of God he created them.

GENESIS 1:27, NRSV

Prayer recovers the shape of our creation. We are created in "the image of God." We are declared, on the authority of Genesis, "good." We, and everyone and everything around us has this basic beauty, this wondrous goodness. But we very often don't feel at all good. We do not perceive ourselves "in the image of God." We are conscious of failure and inadequacy; we experience criticism and rejection; we feel lousy. The memory of our good creation is obscured in a thick fog of failure and inadequacy.

Prayer is a reentry into the reality of our good creation.

ANSWERING GOD

FAMILY OF FAITH

Happy are the people who know the festal shout,
who walk, O LORD, in the light of your countenance.

PSALM 89:15, NRSV

The gospel is never for individuals but always for a people. Sin fragments us, separates us, and sentences us to solitary confinement. Gospel restores us, unites us, and sets us in community.

The life of faith revealed and nurtured in the biblical narratives is highly personal but never merely individual: always there is a family, a tribe, a nation—*church*. God's love and salvation are revealed and experienced in the congregation of the people "who know the festal shout."

REVERSED THUNDER

GOD SHARES OUR LIFE

All day we parade God's praise—
we thank you by name over and over.

PSALM 44:8, THE MESSAGE

Everything we learn about God through
Scripture and in Christ tells us that he knows
what it is like to change a diaper for the thirteenth
time in the day. To see a report over which we have
worked long and carefully gather dust on
somebody's desk for weeks and weeks. . . .

A book on God has for its title *The God Who
Stands, Stoops, and Stays.* That summarizes the
posture of blessing: God stands—he is foundational
and dependable; God stoops—he kneels to our
level and meets us where we are; God stays—he
sticks with us through hard times and good, sharing
his life with us in grace and peace.

A LONG OBEDIENCE

BREAD AND WINE

"This is my body, which is given for you.
Do this in remembrance of me."

LUKE 22:19, NRSV

Jesus was fond of using the common setting of meals, dinners, and wedding suppers both for telling stories and engaging in conversation. . . .

We know that Jesus worshiped in synagogues and temple, the standard places where God was worshiped and Scripture taught. But most of his teaching and prayer took place in streets and fields, on the mountains and in the homes where he gave and was given meals. When he established a way for his followers to maintain what they had experienced, received, and been commanded by him to do, he did it by telling them to have a meal together of bread and wine. They did it. And we keep doing it.

REVERSED THUNDER

WHOLE RELATIONSHIPS

When someone gives you a hard time,
respond with the energies of prayer, for then you are
working out of . . . your God-created selves.

MATTHEW 5:44, THE MESSAGE

The personal relationships for which we were created and in which we are confused because of our sin, are re-created (redeemed) by salvation.

Salvation is the act of God in which we are rescued from the consequences of our sin (bondage, fragmentation) and put in a position to live in free, open, loving relationships with God and our neighbors. The double command "love God . . . love your neighbor . . ." assumes salvation as a background. *Without* God's act of salvation we are "dead in trespasses and sin." *With* God's act of salvation we are able to be addressed by a whole series of commands by which we are ordered into live, whole, healthy relationships with God and other persons.

FIVE SMOOTH STONES

GOD'S POWER

He's GOD, our God, in charge of the whole earth.

PSALM 105:7, THE MESSAGE

What is better for the nation? To encourage 200 million citizens to assert themselves (which in practice means the assertion of greed and ambition)? Or, believing that God is already asserting a far better will in countless visible and invisible ways in a complex working out of salvation in every level of economy and society and culture, to put myself at the disposal of that will because "power belongs to God."

Prayer is action that builds a bridge across the chasm of self-assertion to a life of humanity, which means getting more interested in and excited about what God is doing than in figuring out what I can do to express myself or improve the world.

WHERE YOUR TREASURE IS

THE WORK OF SPIRITUALITY

God is doing what is best for us,
training us to live God's holy best.

HEBREWS 12:10, THE MESSAGE

The work of spirituality is to recognize where we are—the particular circumstances of our lives—to recognize grace and say, "Do you suppose God wants to be with me in a way that does not involve changing my spouse or getting rid of my spouse or my kids, but in changing me, and doing something in my life that maybe I could never experience without this pain and this suffering?"

Sometimes I think all I do as pastor is speak the word "God" in a situation in which it hasn't been said before, where people haven't recognized his presence.

THE CONTEMPLATIVE PASTOR

CHOOSING PRAYER

I call out to High God,
the God who holds me together.

PSALM 57:3, THE MESSAGE

In the Jesus wilderness story our Lord learned to discern between religion that uses God and spirituality that enters into what God does, and he was thereby prepared to be our Savior, not merely our helper or adviser or entertainer.

In the David wilderness story we see a young man hated and hunted like an animal, . . . forced to decide between a life of blasphemy and a life of prayer—and choosing prayer. In choosing prayer he entered into the practice of holiness. A very earthy holiness it was, but holiness all the same.

LEAP OVER A WALL

STEADFAST LOVE

The steadfast love of the LORD never ceases,
his mercies never come to an end; they are new
every morning; great is thy faithfulness.

LAMENTATIONS 3:22–23, RSV

The five poem-prayers in Lamentations . . . express the suffering God's people experienced during and after the fall of Jerusalem, the most devastating disaster in their history. At the very center of this dark time, and placed at almost the exact center of these five poems . . . is this verse: "The steadfast love of the LORD never ceases, his mercies never come to an end. . . ."

God's persistence is not a dogged repetition of duty. It has all the surprise and creativity, and yet all the certainty and regularity, of a new day. Sunrise—when the spontaneous and the certain arrive at the same time.

RUN WITH THE HORSES

THE LIFE OF HISTORY

God . . . doesn't play hide-and-seek with us.
He's not remote; he's near. We live and move in him.

ACTS 17:27–28, THE MESSAGE

History tumbles out a mass of data—wars, famines, murders, and accidents—along with sunrises and still waters, lilies of the field and green pastures. God's people have been convinced that it is possible in prayer and praise, in listening and believing, to discern meaning in this apparent chaos and therefore to read good news in the daily life of history. The means by which this is done is through the proclamation of Jesus Christ, the Lamb slain from the foundation of the world.

We do not need Christ to tell us that the world is full of trouble. But we do need his explanation of history if its troubles are not to be meaningless. In his life, death, and resurrection history comes to focus.

REVERSED THUNDER

GOD KNEELS AMONG US

May GOD of Zion bless you—
GOD who made heaven and earth!

PSALM 134:3, THE MESSAGE

God enters into covenant with us, he pours out his own life for us, he shares the goodness of his Spirit, the vitality of his creation, the joys of his redemption. He empties himself among us, and we get what he is. That is *blessing*.

God gets down on his knees among us, gets on our level and shares himself with us. He does not reside afar off and send us diplomatic messages. He kneels among us. . . . God shares himself generously and graciously.

A LONG OBEDIENCE

SONGS EVERYWHERE

*I'm whistling, laughing, and jumping
for joy; I'm singing your song, High God.*

PSALM 9:2, THE MESSAGE

Worship sings.

There are songs everywhere in Scripture. The people of God sing. They express exuberance in realizing the majesty of God and the mercy of Christ, the wholeness of reality and their new-found ability to participate in it. Songs proliferate. Hymns gather the voices of men, women, and children into century-tiered choirs. Moses sings. Miriam sings. Deborah sings. David sings. Mary sings. Angels sing. Jesus and his disciples sing. Paul and Silas sing. When persons of faith become aware of who God is and what he does they sing. The songs are irrepressible.

REVERSED THUNDER

*Our beliefs
shape our behavior.*

GOD'S WILL IS DONE

Your love, GOD, fills the earth!
Train me to live by your counsel.

PSALM 119:64, THE MESSAGE

Taking into account the rebellious passions . . . and slothful wills of millions of people, along with the good intentions, misguided helpfulness and ill-timed ventures of other millions—not to speak of the disciplined love . . . and sacrificial service of still other millions—our Sovereign presides over and works with all of this material, personal and political. With it and out of it he shapes existence. He seems to be in no hurry. But prayer discerns that leisure is not indolence. Slowness is not slackness. In the end the sovereign will is done.

WHERE YOUR TREASURE IS

FREE LIFE OF FAITH

God's law is not something alien, imposed on us from without, but woven into the very fabric of our creation.

ROMANS 2:15, THE MESSAGE

Moses climbed the mountain to receive God's revelation. He returned with the Ten Commandments, the constitution and bill of rights for a people who were then to live the free life of faith. Some people mistakenly look at those commandments as restrictive, not realizing that for those who first heard them (and for those who even now hear them in faith) they provided for and preserved the values of the free life. The reality and truth of God is protected from commercialization and manipulation. Human life is honored. The dignity of work is protected. Close, personal relationships are preserved. Truth is respected.

TRAVELING LIGHT

THE PRESENCE OF GOD

GOD sticks by all who love him.

PSALM 145:20, THE MESSAGE

D avid entered the Valley of Elah with a God-dominated, not a Goliath-dominated, imagination. He was incredulous that everyone was cowering before this infidel giant. . . .

Tending his father's sheep, David . . . had experienced God's strength in protecting the sheep in his fights with lions and bears. He had practiced the presence of God so thoroughly that God's word, which he couldn't literally hear, was far more real to him than the lion's roar, which he could hear.

His praying and singing, his meditation and adoration had shaped an imagination in him that set each sheep and lamb, bear and lion into something large and vast and robust: God.

LEAP OVER A WALL

MADE RIGHT

*Since we are justified by faith, we have peace
with God through our Lord Jesus Christ.*

ROMANS 5:1, NRSV

Justification means being put together the way we
are supposed to be. Made right—not improved,
not decorated, not veneered, not patched up, but
justified. Our fundamental being is set in right
relationship with God. . . .

We are never right in ourselves, but only in
response to and as a result of God working in
and through us. We can never be justified apart
from God, but only in some kind of communion
with him.

Therefore we must have faith, for faith is the
personal relationship supreme. Justification is not
coercive; it comes by faith, the willing responsiveness
and involvement of a free person.

TRAVELING LIGHT

CREATIVE IN CHRIST

GOD is solid backing to a well-lived life.

PROVERBS 10:29, THE MESSAGE

E veryone is born to live creatively, but many of us fail to do so. Why? Because we are lazy. Creativity is difficult. When you are being creative, you're living by faith. You don't know what's next because the created, by definition, is what's never been before. So you're living at the edge of something in which you're not very confident. You might fail: in fact, you almost certainly will fail a good part of the time. All the creative persons I know throw away most of the stuff they do.

The streets and fields, the homes and markets of the world are an art gallery displaying not culture, but new creations in Christ.

THE CONTEMPLATIVE PASTOR

PRAYING IN THIS PLACE

"How could we sing the
LORD's song in a foreign land?"

PSALM 137:4, NRSV

"How can we sing the Lord's song in a strange land?" The Israelites didn't think they could. But they did. My, how they did! How did they do it? . . . They immersed themselves in torah-meditation: before they knew it they were praying. They were trees. Transplanted to Babylon they put down roots, put out leaves, and produced fruit.

We all suppose that we could pray, or pray better, if we were in the right place. We put off praying until we are where we think we should be, or want to be. We let our fantasies or our circumstances distract us from attending to the word of God that is aimed right where we are, and invites our answers from that spot.

ANSWERING GOD

SHARING THE SUFFERING

Surely He has borne our griefs and carried our sorrows.

ISAIAH 53:4, NKJV

The biblical revelation neither explains nor eliminates suffering. It shows, rather, God entering into the life of suffering humanity, accepting and sharing the suffering.

Scripture in not a lecture from God, pointing the finger at unfortunate sufferers and saying, "I told you so: here and here and here is where you went wrong; now you are paying for it." Nor is it a program from God providing, step by step, for the gradual elimination of suffering in a series of five-year plans (or, on a grander scale, dispensations). There is no progress from more to less suffering. . . . The suffering is *there*, and where the sufferer is, God is.

FIVE SMOOTH STONES

HOPE OF GOD'S PROMISE

The lines of purpose in your lives
never grow slack, tightly tied as they are to your
future in heaven, kept taut by hope.

COLOSSIANS 1:5, THE MESSAGE

Without hope a person has basically two ways to respond to the future, with wishing or with anxiety. Wishing looks to the future as a fulfillment, usually miraculous, of desire. It expands its energy in daydreaming and fantasy. Anxiety looks to the future as a demonstration of inadequacy—present weakness is projected to the point of disaster.

Hope is a response to the future that has its foundation in the promises of God. It looks at the future as time for the completion of God's promise. It refuses to extrapolate either desire or anxiety into the future, but instead believes that God's promise gives the proper content to it.

LIKE DEW YOUR YOUTH

FREEDOM TO FAIL

It is not what you and I do . . .
it is what God is doing, and he is creating
something totally new, a free life!

GALATIANS 6:16, THE MESSAGE

F ear of failure inhibits freedom; the freedom to fail encourages it. The life of faith encourages the risk taking that frequently results in failure, for it encourages human ventures into crisis and the unknown. When we are in situations where we are untested (like Peter at the arrest of Jesus) or unaccustomed (like Peter on the Mount of Transfiguration), we are sometimes going to fail. . . . These failures, though, are never disasters because they become the means by which we realize new depths of our humanity and new vistas of divine grace. In the midst of our humanity and divine grace, the free life is shaped.

TRAVELING LIGHT

GOD GIVES LAVISHLY

*"If you knew the gift of God,
. . . you would have asked him."*

JOHN 4:10, NRSV

God gives. He is generous; He is lavishly generous.

That is God's way. He did it with his own Son, Jesus. He gave him away. He gave him to the nations. He did not keep him on display. He did not preserve him in a museum. He did not show him off as a trophy. "God so loved the world that he gave his only Son, so that everyone who believes in him may not perish but may have eternal life" (John 3:16, NRSV).

RUN WITH THE HORSES

THE LARGER CONGREGATION

God-friendship is for God-worshipers;
they are the ones he confides in.

PSALM 25:14, THE MESSAGE

E very time we worship our minds are informed, our memories refreshed with the judgments of God. We are familiarized with what God says, what he has decided, the ways he is working out our salvation.

There is simply no place where these can be done as well as in worship. . . . In worship we are part of "the large congregation" where all the writers of Scripture address us.

A LONG OBEDIENCE

PEOPLE WHO PRAISE

Oh blessed be GOD! . . .
He didn't abandon us defenseless.

PSALM 124:6, THE MESSAGE

How God wants us to sing like this! Christians are not fussy moralists who cluck their tongues over a world going to hell; Christians are people who praise the God who is on our side. Christians are not pious pretenders in the midst of a decadent culture; Christians are robust witnesses to the God who is our help. Christians are not fatigued outcasts who carry righteousness as a burden in a world where the wicked flourish; Christians are people who sing "Oh, blessed be GOD! . . . He didn't abandon us defenseless."

A LONG OBEDIENCE

PRACTICED IN PRAYER

He only is my rock and my salvation;
. . . I shall not be moved.

PSALM 62:6, NKJV

The self wants to be excited, entertained, gratified, coddled, reassured, rewarded, challenged, indulged. There are people on hand to manipulate and market these impulses by seduction and persuasion.

The American self characteristically chooses advertisers instead of apostles as guides. Self-assertion is, in fact, a euphemism for a way of life dominated by impulse and pressure. The self is alternately moved from within by whatever occurs in the emotions and glands, from without by whatever is presented by fashion and fad. As we become practiced in prayer we are unmoved by such bagatelles.

WHERE YOUR TREASURE IS

RUNNING TO GOD

God delivers generous love, he makes good on his word.

PSALM 57:5, THE MESSAGE

While Saul was the occasion for David's being in the wilderness, Saul neither defined nor dominated the wilderness. The wilderness was full of God, not Saul.

Wilderness, in itself, makes nothing happen. Saul and David were both in the wilderness. Saul was running after David, obsessed with hunting him down, his life narrowed to a murderous squint. Meanwhile, David was running to God and finding himself in his God-refuge praying, wide eyed in wonder, taking in the glory, awake and ready for God's generous love, for the God who "makes good on his word."

LEAP OVER A WALL

SACRIFICIAL OFFERING

O LORD, in the morning, thou dost
hear my voice: in the morning I prepare
a sacrifice for thee, and watch.

PSALM 5:3, RSV

A sacrifice is the material means of assembling a life before God in order to let God work with it. Sacrifice isn't something we do for God, but simply setting out the stuff of life for him to do something with.

On the altar the sacrificial offering is changed into what is pleasing and acceptable to God. In the act of offering we give up ownership and control, and watch to see what God will do with it. With a deep awareness that the God who speaks life into us also listens when we speak, we put into words the difficulties and delights that we foresee in the hours ahead. We assemble fears and hopes, apprehensions and anticipations, and place them on the altar as an offering: "I prepare a sacrifice, and watch."

ANSWERING GOD

GOD SPEAKS

*Oh yes, he's our God, . . . drop everything
and listen, listen as he speaks.*

PSALM 95:7–8, THE MESSAGE

The Scriptures are a mixed blessing because the
moment the words are written they are in
danger of losing the living resonance of the spoken
word and reduced to something that is looked at,
studied, interpreted, but not heard personally. . . .

God speaks, declaring his creation and his
salvation so that we might believe, that is, trustingly
participate in his creation of us, his salvation of us.
The intent of revelation is not to inform us about
God but to involve us in God.

REVERSED THUNDER

FORGIVENESS

If someone falls into sin, forgivingly restore him. . . .
You might be needing forgiveness before the day's out.

GALATIANS 6:1, THE MESSAGE

T he act of forgiveness begins by accepting the sin, whatever it is. It does not blink at the sin. . . . It does not excuse or modify or explain it: it faces it. And it accepts the consequences of the sin. Whatever suffering, whatever penalties, whatever discomfort, whatever inconveniences proceed from the sin, they are also accepted. What else was the cross but an act of enormous courage, accepting the results of sin?

Forgiveness proceeds by accepting the person who committed the sin. It aggressively initiates a new movement of love toward that person. It gathers him, or her, back into the relationship of love, saying, "*You* are what is real, not the sin. Nothing you or anyone else can do will separate you from me."

LIKE DEW YOUR YOUTH

MAJESTIC AND HOLY

Fear God. Do what he tells you.

ECCLESIASTES 12:13, THE MESSAGE

"Fear God." *Reverence* might be a better word. *Awe.* The Bible isn't interested in whether we believe in God or not. It assumes that everyone more or less does. What it is interested in is the response we have to him: Will we let God be as he is, majestic and holy, vast and wondrous, or will we always be trying to whittle him down to the size of our small minds, insist on confining him within the boundaries we are comfortable with . . . ?

The Bible talks of the fear of the Lord—not to scare us but to bring us to awesome attention before the overwhelming grandeur of God.

A LONG OBEDIENCE

GOD NEVER GIVES UP

*The vessel he was making of clay was spoiled
in the potter's hand, and he reworked it into another
vessel, as it seemed good to the potter to do.*

JEREMIAH 18:4, RSV

Jeremiah knew all about . . . spoiled vessels—men
and women with impurities and blemishes that
resist the shaping hand of the creator. He rubbed
shoulders daily with people who were not useful:
imperfections made their lives leak, . . . failure . . .
made their lives wobble or tip. . . . Jeremiah had
other words for it: sin, rebellion, self-will. . . .

He continued to observe. What would the
potter do now? Kick the wheel and go off in a sulk?
Throw the clay at the cat and go to the market . . .
? Neither. "He reworked it. . . ." God kneads and
presses, pushes and pulls. The creative work starts
over again, patiently, skillfully. God doesn't give up.

RUN WITH THE HORSES

THE PRICE IS PAID

God sent forth his Son,
born of woman, born under the law, to redeem
those who were under the law.

GALATIANS 4:4–5, RSV

All Paul's readers would have been familiar with the . . . Greek process for freeing slaves. The word *redeem* describes this process. Sometimes a slave caught the attention of a wealthy free person and for some reason or other—compassion, affection, justice—the free person would then go to the temple or shrine and deposit with the priests the sum of money required for manumission. The priests would then deliver an oracle . . . then pass the redemption price on to the recent owner. The ex-slave . . . was free.

That, says Paul, is what has happened to each of us. . . . A price has been paid to free us. We are valuable beyond calculation.

TRAVELING LIGHT

LOVE IN GOD'S KINGDOM

*The person who refuses to love doesn't
know the first thing about God, because God is love.*

1 JOHN 4:8, THE MESSAGE

Worldly wisdom concedes that love is marvelous in the bedroom, but it is convinced that it has no place in government. It expects [declarations] of love on a beach in the moonlight but finds them embarrassingly out of place around the conference table of a corporate board room.

The problem is that nothing in all of biblical literature corroborates that contention. God is not only engaged in loving each person in a saving way, he is bringing a kingdom into being. Moreover, the whole of Scripture tells us that the same God who rules the world saves the soul.

WHERE YOUR TREASURE IS

THE GOD OF THIS PLACE

*Live in such a way that you
are a credit to the Message of Christ.*

PHILIPPIANS 1:27, THE MESSAGE

B eing where we don't want to be with people we
don't want to be with forces a decision: Will I
focus my attention on what is wrong with the
world and feel sorry for myself? Or will I focus my
energies on how I can live at my best in this place
I find myself?

We can say: "I don't like it; I want to be where
I was ten years ago." . . . Or we can say: "I will do
my best with what is here. Far more important than
the climate of this place, the economics of this place,
the neighbors in this place, is the God of this place.
God is here with me. . . . It is just as possible to live
out the will of God here as any place else."

RUN WITH THE HORSES

THE FREEDOM TO LOVE

Love . . . puts up with anything,
trusts God always, always looks for the best.

1 CORINTHIANS 13:7, THE MESSAGE

The freedom that comes from a life of faith has a quietness and a naturalness to it. It is not assertive or ostentatious. . . .

I don't think that we discover this primarily in the passionate acts of love that immerse us in a sea of ecstasy. For the most part we must not look for it in the dramatic, in the parade, or in the honeymoon. We must express it in the minute decisions we make in regard to our feelings and gestures and words. . . .

At the last minute, as it were, when everything else has done its work and made its contribution, there is the freedom to change a tone of voice, to write a sentence in a letter, to make a telephone call—the freedom to love.

TRAVELING LIGHT

BIBLICAL ANCESTORS

GOD, your name is eternal,
. . . you'll never be out-of-date.

PSALM 135:13, THE MESSAGE

What would we think of a pollster who issued a definitive report . . . if we discovered later that he had interviewed only one person . . . ? We would dismiss the conclusions as frivolous. Yet that is exactly the kind of evidence too many Christians accept as the final truth about much more important matters—such as answered prayer, . . . and eternal salvation. The only person they consult is themselves, and the only experience they evaluate is the most recent ten minutes.

We need other experiences, . . . the centuries of experience provided by our biblical ancestors. A Christian who has David in his bones, and Paul in his fingertips . . . will know how much and how little value to put on his own momentary feelings.

A LONG OBEDIENCE

NEW EVERY MORNING

The steadfast love of the LORD
never ceases, his mercies never come to an end,
they are new every morning.

LAMENTATIONS 3:22–23, NRSV

We have a finite number of ways to sin; God has an infinite number of ways to forgive. After observing the human condition for a few years, we find that in regard to sin we're mostly watching reruns. After a while we find that people pretty much do the same old thing generation after generation.

Sinning doesn't take much imagination. But forgiveness and salvation? That's a different story: every time it happens, it's fresh, original, catching us by surprise. Sin isn't creative work, and the more we're around it, the duller it seems. Salvation, in contrast, is "new every morning."

LEAP OVER A WALL

DOORSTEP OF PRAISE

I bless GOD every chance I get;
my lungs expand with his praise.

PSALM 34:1, THE MESSAGE

All prayer, pursued far enough, becomes praise. Any prayer, no matter how desperate its origin, no matter how angry and fearful the experiences it traverses, ends up in praise. It does not always get there quickly or easily—the trip can take a lifetime—but the end is always praise. . . .

No matter how much we suffer, no matter our doubts, no matter how angry we get, no matter how many times we have asked in desperation or doubt, "How long?", prayer develops finally into praise. Everything finds its way to the doorstep of praise. Praise is the consummating prayer.

ANSWERING GOD

JESUS CALLS SINNERS

*Christ brought us together
through his death on the Cross.*

EPHESIANS 2:16, THE MESSAGE

Churches are not Victorian parlors where everything is always picked up and ready for guests. They are messy family rooms.

They are not show rooms. They are living rooms, and if the persons living in them are sinners, there are going to be clothes scattered about, handprints on the woodwork, and mud on the carpet. For as long as Jesus insists on calling sinners and not the righteous to repentance—and there is no indication as yet that he has changed his policy in that regard—churches are going to be an embarrassment to the fastidious and an affront to the upright.

They are places, locations, where the light of Christ is shown. They are not themselves in the light.

REVERSED THUNDER

ENJOYING GOD

I lift you high in praise, my God, O my King!

PSALM 145:1, THE MESSAGE

God is personal reality to be enjoyed. We are so created and so redeemed that we are capable of enjoying him. All the movements of discipleship arrive at a place where joy is experienced. Every step of assent toward God develops the capacity to enjoy. Not only is there, increasingly, more to be enjoyed, there is steadily the acquired ability to enjoy it. Best of all, we don't have to wait until we get to the end of the road before we enjoy what is at the end of the road.

A LONG OBEDIENCE

CHRIST TRIUMPHANT

*The LORD sends forth from Zion your
mighty scepter. Rule in the midst of your foes!*

PSALM 110:2, RSV

The only way to understand history is to begin, openly and firmly, with Christ. . . . He is the Alpha in the alphabet of historical discourse. He is not an afterthought brought in as a rescue operation. . . .

The favorite psalm in the early Christian community was the Psalm 110: 2, 5: "The LORD sends forth from Zion your mighty scepter. Rule in the midst of your foes! . . . The LORD is at your right hand; he will shatter kings on the day of his wrath." Biblical Christians do not sentimentalize Christ. There is fierceness and militancy here. The world is in conflict; our Christ is the first on the field of battle. High issues are decided every day. Christ is not only worshipped each Sunday, he is triumphant each week day.

REVERSED THUNDER

GOD'S DOESN'T LEAVE US

Thank GOD! He deserves
your thanks. His love never quits.

PSALM 136:1, THE MESSAGE

When we sin and mess up our lives, we find that God doesn't go off and leave us—he enters into our trouble and saves us. That is good. . . . We discover reasons and motivations for living in faith and find that God is already helping us to do it—and that is good. Praise God!

"A Christian," wrote Augustine, "should be an alleluia from head to foot." . . . That is the truth of our lives. God made us, redeems us, provides for us. The natural, . . . logical response to that is praise to God.

A LONG OBEDIENCE

GOD HAS THE FIRST WORD

God, listen to me shout, bend an ear to my prayer.

PSALM 61:1, THE MESSAGE

We want life on our conditions, not on God's conditions. Praying puts us at risk of getting involved in God's conditions. Be slow to pray. Praying most often doesn't give get us what we want but what God wants, something quite at variance with what we conceive to be in our best interests. And when we realize what is going on, it is often too late to go back. Be slow to pray.

Prayer is never the first word; it is always it the second word. God has the first word.

WORKING THE ANGLES

AUGUST

Prayer is a
focus upon God.

CHANGED BY WORSHIP

So come, let us worship; bow before him,
on your knees before GOD, who made us!

PSALM 95:6, THE MESSAGE

Worship does not satisfy our hunger for God—it whets our appetite. Our need for God is not taken care of by engaging in worship—it deepens. It overflows the hour and permeates the week. The need is expressed in a desire for peace and security. Our everyday needs are changed by the act of worship. We are no longer living from hand to mouth, greedily scrambling through the human rat race to make the best we can out of a mean existence. Our basic needs suddenly become worthy of the dignity of creatures made in the image of God.

A LONG OBEDIENCE

SUBORDINATE TO GOD

*If you prefer father or mother
over me, you don't deserve me.*

MATTHEW 10:37, THE MESSAGE

We become aware of God's grand sovereignty in prayer; we also discover a developing inclination to obedience. Slowly but surely, not culture, not family, not government, not job, not even the tyrannous self can stand against the quiet power and creative influence of God's sovereignty. Every natural tie of family and race, every willed commitment to person and nation is finally subordinated to the rule of God.

WHERE YOUR TREASURE IS

BREAD AND SWORD

Your words are so choice, so tasty;
I prefer them to the best home cooking.

PSALM 119:103, THE MESSAGE

David came to the sanctuary without food for his stomach and without a weapon in his hand. He left with a full stomach and girded for strenuous battle.

A sanctuary isn't only a place where my . . . connection with God is sharpened; it's also where I, like David, get bread and a sword. . . . God's word is bread; Gods word is a sword. . . . When we're pushed to the boundaries of our existence, . . . we seek sanctuary, a holy place. And then this wonderful surprise. . . . We enter weakened and endangered and before we know it are strengthened and equipped to face danger.

LEAP OVER A WALL

BEGIN WITH ACCEPTANCE

We will not compare ourselves with each other as
if one of us were better and another worse. We have
far more interesting things to do with our lives.

GALATIANS 5:26, THE MESSAGE

Our partial acceptances of one another . . . are
in fact, rejections. Acceptance is a carrot
held out to motivate us to conform, not a gift to set
us free. "If you will dress this way, or talk this way,
or behave this way . . . you will be accepted as one
of us." But, however earnestly and politely these
conditions are set forth, they are rejections. . . .

The gospel reverses that process; it begins
with acceptance, then, with the rush of freedom
into the soul that brings, the spiritual, moral,
responsible life develops.

TRAVELING LIGHT

PAYING ATTENTION

When you come before God
. . . find a quiet, secluded place.

MATTHEW 6:5–6, THE MESSAGE

I t takes time to develop a life of prayer: set-aside, disciplined, deliberate time. It isn't accomplished on the run. I know I can't be busy and pray at the same time. I can be active and pray; but I cannot be *busy* and pray. I cannot be inwardly rushed, distracted, or dispersed.

In order to pray I have to be paying more attention to God than to what people are saying to me, to God than to my clamoring ego. Usually, for that to happen there must be a deliberate withdrawal from the noise of the day, a disciplined detachment from the insatiable self.

THE CONTEMPLATIVE PASTOR

GOD SAYS "YES"

Jesus Christ, whom we preached among you . . . was
not Yes and No; but in him it is always Yes. For all
the promises of God find their Yes in him. That is why
we utter the Amen through him to the glory of God.

2 CORINTHIANS 1:19–20, RSV

That word ["yes"] expresses, perhaps better than any other, the gospel message. God says "yes" to humanity. Humanity returns the "yes.". . .

Yes in Hebrew is *Amen.* It is rich and allusive in meaning. It indicates firmness, solidity. It describes what is nailed down. God is "Amen" (Isa. 65:16)—sure, faithful, affirmative. Because God is "Amen," people can live in "Amen," that is, in faith. We are taught to say "yes" to the God who says "yes" to us in Christ and so be connected in an affirmative way with the God who has redeemed us.

FIVE SMOOTH STONES

THE WORLD OF WORK

Go . . . and make disciples of all nations. . . .

MATTHEW 28:19, RSV

When Jesus said, "Go . . . and make disciples of all nations, baptizing them in the name of the Father and of the Son and of the Holy Spirit, teaching them to observe all that I have commanded you; and lo, I am with you always, to the close of the age"(Matt. 28:19–20, RSV), he wasn't giving a job description for the Christian but saying something about the stance a Christian takes into the world of work. If we don't see how everyday work in some way or another is a response to the command "Go . . . and make disciples," we are going to become either very discontented with the meaning and worth of our work, or else very careless and blasé about our obedience to Christ.

LIKE DEW YOUR YOUTH

WE WILL BE LIKE HIM

Beloved, we are God's children now; what we will be has not yet been revealed. What we do know is this; when he is revealed, we will be like him.

1 JOHN 3:2, NRSV

We are children; we *will be* adults. We can see what we are now; we are children of God. We don't yet see the results of what we are becoming, but we know the goal, to be like Christ, or, in Paul's words, to arrive at "maturity, to the measure of the full stature of Christ" (Eph 4:13, NRSV).

We do not deteriorate. We do not disintegrate. We *become.*

RUN WITH THE HORSES

A REDEMPTIVE LIFE

Ask and you'll get; seek and you'll find;
knock and the door will open.

LUKE 11:9, THE MESSAGE

God presents himself to us in the history of Jesus Christ as a servant. With that before us it is easy to assume the role of master and begin ordering him around. But God is not a servant to be called into action when we are too tired to do something ourselves, not an expert to be called on when we find we are not equipped to handle a specialized problem in living. God did not become a servant so that we could order him around but so that we could join him in a redemptive life.

A LONG OBEDIENCE

BELIEFS SHAPE BEHAVIOR

A mindful person relishes wisdom.

PROVERBS 10:23, THE MESSAGE

One of the great lies of the age is that what I believe is nobody's business but my own, that what I do in the secrecy of my own heart is of no account to anyone else. But what I believe is everybody's business precisely because what goes on in my heart very soon shapes the way I act in society. . . .

Our beliefs are not off-the-cuff answers we give to an opinion survey; our beliefs are the deepest things about us. Our beliefs shape our behavior; therefore our beliefs are the most practical thing about us.

WHERE YOUR TREASURE IS

THE DIGNITY OF DAVID'S LIFE

Why are you down in the dumps, dear soul? . . .
Fix my eyes on God—soon I'll be praising again.

PSALM 42:5, THE MESSAGE

David, who lived exuberantly, also lamented fiercely. . . .

Seventy percent of the Psalms are laments. These laments either originate in or derive from the praying life of David. David repeatedly faced loss, disappointment, death. But he neither avoided, denied, nor soft-pedaled any of those difficulties. He faced everything and he prayed everything. David's laments are part and parcel of the craggy majesty and towering dignity of his life.

LEAP OVER A WALL

OUR CREATOR

*GOD made the heavens—royal splendor radiates
from him, a powerful beauty sets him apart.*

PSALM 96:5, THE MESSAGE

E verything is created. Everything carries within
its form and texture the signature of its
Creator. No part of this material world is
unconnected with God; every cell is in the organism
of salvation. Biblical religion cannot be lived apart
from matter—the seen, felt, tasted, smelled, and
listened to creation. . . .

Nothing merely happened along. Chokecherries
and tundra and weasels are not random accidents.
Since everything is by design, no part of creation
can be bypassed if we intend to live in the fullest
possible relation to our Creator in his creation.

ANSWERING GOD

COMPLETE REVELATION

"I am the Alpha and the Omega, the first and the last, the beginning and the end."

REVELATION 22:13, RSV

I n the first chapter of the Revelation God identifies himself with the sentence, "I am the Alpha and the Omega" (Rev. 1:8). In the final vision this is expanded to "I am the Alpha and the Omega, the first and the last, the beginning and the end" (Rev. 22:13).

Alpha is the first letter in the Greek alphabet; Omega is the last. Alpha and Omega include between them all the letters. Anything written must use the letters of the alphabet. God is all the letters of the alphabet. All that is written comes from who God is. A revealing God who is complete in himself has given us a revelation of himself which is now complete.

REVERSED THUNDER

RELATIONSHIPS OF GRACE

The command we have from Christ
is blunt: Loving God includes loving people.

1 JOHN 4:21, THE MESSAGE

We are faced, daily, with the reality that something has gone wrong with our families. Our children fight and quarrel; our parenting misfires. We are involved in failure, and we feel guilty.

Something *has*, of course, gone wrong with the family, but it went wrong long before we came on the scene. It is futile to complain or feel guilty. We can, though, go to work and nurture family life on the new grounds provided by the Holy Spirit. Blood relationships are transformed into relationships of grace. Our natural families are informed and redeemed by the same principles that are foundational in the community of the Holy Spirit, the church.

LIKE DEW YOUR YOUTH

HAPPINESS THAT LASTS

GOD is good to one and all;
everything he does is suffused with grace.

PSALM 145:9, THE MESSAGE

Everyone wants to be happy, to be blessed. Too many people are willfully refusing to pay attention to the One who wills our happiness and ignorantly supposing that the Christian way is a harder way to get what they want than in doing it on their own. They are wrong. God's ways and God's presence are where we experience the happiness that lasts.

A LONG OBEDIENCE

BECOMING WHOLE

Let us work for the benefit of all, starting with the people closest to us in the community of faith.

GALATIANS 6:10, THE MESSAGE

Some people come to church looking for a way to make life better, to feel good about themselves. . . . Other people come to church because they want God to save and rule them. . . .

One group of people sees religion as a way to successful happy living; nothing that interferes with the success or interrupts the happiness will be tolerated. The other group sees religion as a way in which hurt, flawed, and damaged persons become whole in relation to God; anything will be accepted (mockery, pain, renunciaton, self-denial) in order to deepen and extend that reality.

One . . . is the way of enhancing what I want; the other way is a commitment of myself to become what God wants.

RUN WITH THE HORSES

INTIMACY WITH GOD

Because you are sons, God has sent the Spirit
of his Son into our hearts, crying, "Abba! Father!"

GALATIANS 4:6, RSV

A*bba* is an Aramaic word, . . . the native speech of Jesus. Abba means Father, but in a colloquial, intimate sense. The nearest equivalent in our language is Daddy, or perhaps Papa.

In Christ we are introduced into an unprecedented intimacy with God. Nowhere in the Old Testament do we find God addressed as Father. . . . But Jesus always addressed God in this way in his prayers. . . . The gift of sonship confers the privilege of the child to address the father with intimacy.

TRAVELING LIGHT

BIBLICAL LOVE

"This is how much God loved the world:
he gave his Son, his one and only Son."

JOHN 3:16, THE MESSAGE

World and self are the double foci of God's love. God does not have one form of action for the world and another for individuals. God does not deal with the soul on the basis of personal love and with the nation on the basis of impersonal expediency. . . . It is love both times.

It is quite true that the expressions of love in society . . . require different forms from those within families. The usual form in which love comes to expression in the public sector is a passion for justice. Legislation rather than kisses, the vigorous pursuit of policy rather than . . . a dozen roses. . . . But what must not change is the biblical base of love.

WHERE YOUR TREASURE IS

LISTENING TO GOD

*"There is in my heart as it were a burning
fire shut up in my bones, and I am weary with
holding it in, and I cannot."*

JEREMIAH 20:9, RSV

Jeremiah did not commission a public opinion
survey to find out what the Jerusalem crowds
wanted to hear about God. He did not ask for a
show of hands to determine what level of moral
behavior to stress.

God shaped his behavior. God directed his
life. God trained his perceptions. This shaping and
directing and training took place as he listened to
God and spoke to God. He meditated long and
passionately on the word of God. . . . He wanted
to participate in all that God does.

RUN WITH THE HORSES

FREE TO CREATE

Live creatively, friends.

GALATIANS 6:1, THE MESSAGE

I believe that we are made in the image of God and that because God is a creator, we are creators.

Our early experience often does not encourage that. We are instructed to stay within the lines. In school and church, at home and at work, we are handed someone else's outline and told to learn, pray, play, work—whatever—within it. The intimidation is appallingly successful.

In Christ we are set free to create. He sets us free to live—toward God, with people, in the world—as artists, not as copiers. He sets us free to use the stuff that God gives us to live something original.

TRAVELING LIGHT

MEMORY FOR WHAT WORKS

*GOD, teach me lessons for living
so I can stay the course.*

PSALM 119:33, THE MESSAGE

Biblical history is a good memory for what doesn't work. It is also a good memory for what does work—like remembering what you put in a soup that made it taste so good so you can repeat and enjoy the recipe on another day.

A Christian with a defective memory has to start everything from scratch and spends far too much of his or her time backtracking. . . . A Christian with a good memory avoids repeating old sins, knows the easiest way through complex situations, and instead of starting over each day continues what was begun in Adam.

A LONG OBEDIENCE

GOD OF MERCY

I cry out loudly to GOD,
loudly I plead with GOD for mercy.

PSALM 142:1, THE MESSAGE

As David was leaving Jerusalem, fleeing for his life during Absalom's coup, Shimei walked along a ridge above the road David was taking, throwing rocks and yelling curses (2 Sam. 16:5–14).

The . . . curses brought David to himself. He realized what he had become—all the wrongs he had committed, all the people he had failed. He could have taken a defensive and vengeful posture, but he didn't. He faced the truth that his basic identity wasn't "king" but "sinner" and that he could live only by God's mercy.

He let the suffering bring him into the presence of the God of mercy and grace and love.

LEAP OVER A WALL

COMPLETE VICTORY

Now God has us where he wants us, with all the time in this world and the next to shower grace and kindness upon us.

EPHESIANS 2:7, THE MESSAGE

In the church we are always in process of being affirmed. We find those parts of our lives that are working well, and discovering them gives zest, confidence, and assurance. We are always in process of being corrected. . . . There is a relentless quality to the word of God that insists that we face up to our sloth, our pride, our avarice—all the things that separate us from God's complete victory in us.

And we are in process of being motivated. . . . The motivation to live strenuously for a lifetime must be adequate to sustain us through every shadowed valley and every parched wilderness. The promise of eternal life, and only the promise of eternal life, is sufficient to provide such motivation.

REVERSED THUNDER

NO ILLUSIONS

He got us out of the mess we're in and
restored us to where he always wanted us to be.
And he did it by means of Jesus Christ.

ROMANS 3:25, THE MESSAGE

Christians, for the most part, are the very persons in our society who can be counted on to have no illusions about the depth of depravity in themselves or in the world at large. No other community of people has insisted so consistently through the centuries on calling evil by its right name. No other community has so mercilessly exposed its rationalizations, nor so courageously confessed its own complicity. With admitted expectations, the faith community knows more about what is wrong with the world than any other, and is, at the same time, less cynical or despairing about it.

REVERSED THUNDER

THE WORD GOD SPEAKS

Christ loved the church and gave himself
up for her, in order to make her holy . . . with the
washing of water by the word.

EPHESIANS 5:25–26, NRSV

S t. John in his Gospel describes the Christ as the
Word. More than any other Gospel writer,
he presents us with the Christ *speaking*. Biblical
faith is not guesswork in a moral-spiritual fog; it is
response to an exact word spoken in Jesus Christ.
The Bible begins with God speaking, speaking into
existence first creation and then redemption. The
speaking develops into conversation as people
respond (pray), using their precious gift of speech.
The word God speaks is important; the word we
speak is important. Both words are uttered in the
speech of Jesus Christ.

REVERSED THUNDER

PRESERVED FROM EVIL

Lead us not into temptation,
but deliver us from evil.

MATTHEW 6:13, RSV

No literature is more realistic and honest in facing the harsh facts of life than the Bible. At no time is there the faintest suggestion that the life of faith exempts us from difficulties. What it promises is preservation from all the evil in them.

On every page of the Bible there is recognition that faith encounters troubles. The sixth petition in the Lord's Prayer is "Lead us not into temptation, but deliver us from evil." That prayer is answered every day, sometimes many times a day, in the lives of those who walk in the way of faith.

A LONG OBEDIENCE

WORSHIP IS AFFIRMING

And the four living creatures said,
"Amen!" and the elders fell down and worshiped.

REVELATION 5:14, RSV

A*men* means "yes." It is the worshiping affirmation to the God who affirms us. God says "yes" to us. We respond to his *yes* by saying, "Yes, amen." Worship is affirming.

The end result of the act of worship is that our lives are turned around. We come to God with a history of nay-saying, of rejecting and being rejected. At the throne of God we are immersed in God's "yes," a "yes" that silences all our "no's" and calls forth an answering yes in us.

REVERSED THUNDER

GOD'S RULE

"Beauty" and "holy" mark your
palace rule, GOD, to the very end of time.

PSALM 93:5, THE MESSAGE

God, it seems, does not abandon his essential character when he rules. A God of steadfast love and deep holiness, he is more himself than ever in his rule. He does not set aside the robes of holy love when he exercises his rule in the mud of human history. The *means* of God's rule are consistent with the *ends* of that rule: *holiness*, the gradual, patient, penetrating beauty of God's rule in our desecrated, violated, profaned world.

WHERE YOUR TREASURE IS

POIGNANCY AND POWER

*"Why are you looking for the Living One
in a cemetery? He is not here, but raised up."*

LUKE 24:5, THE MESSAGE

Jesus knew he was dying long before he actually died. He deliberately set out for Jerusalem knowing that death by crucifixion was being prepared for him. A slow death, full of pain. All the while he was doing that he exhibited in word and presence a wonderful vitality, beauty, and faith. There were celebrations with hosannas, conversations full of hope and promise, painful confrontations, tender acts of sacrificial love. The imminence of death didn't cancel out the revelation of God in Jesus but rather gave it added poignancy and power. And resurrection confirmed it.

LEAP OVER A WALL

LIGHT OF THE WORLD

*The city has no need of sun or moon
to shine on it, for the glory of God is its light.*

REVELATION 21:23, NRSV

Christians believe that the light we perceive
and follow in Christ conquers darkness.

St. John's heavenly vision affirms this: "the
glory (*doxa*) of God is its light . . . and night (*nux*)
shall be no more" (Rev. 21:23; 22:5). But there is
more here than the affirmation of light and the
disposition of night. The city is founded on twelve
precious stones, and these stones go beyond merely
affirming the light: they show its plenitude. Light
is a gathering of colors; the stones separate the
colors and hold them up, one by one, for emphasis
and praise.

REVERSED THUNDER

BRIMMING WITH MERCY

Every word you give me is a miracle word—
how could I help but obey?

PSALM 119:129, THE MESSAGE

The Bible provides the revelation of a world that has primarily to do with God. It is a huge world, far larger than what we inhabit on our own. We live in sin-cramped conditions, mostly conscious of ourselves—our feelings and frustrations, our desires and ideas, our achievements and discoveries, our failures and hurts. The Bible is deep and wide with God's love and grace, brimming over with surprises of mercy and mystery.

A LONG OBEDIENCE

God intends good

for us.

HEAVEN-DWELLING GOD

I look to you, heaven-dwelling God,
look up to you for help.

PSALM 123:1, THE MESSAGE

If we want to understand God, we must do it on his terms. If we want to see God the way he really is, we must look to the place of authority—to Scripture and to Jesus Christ.

And do we really want it any other way? I don't think so. We would very soon become contemptuous of a god whom we could figure out like a puzzle or learn to use like a tool. No, if God is worth our attention at all, he must be a God we can look up to—a God we *must* look up to: "I look to you, heaven-dwelling God."

A LONG OBEDIENCE

TRIED AND TRUE

*God is in the midst of her, she shall
not be moved; God will help her right early.*

PSALM 46:5, RSV

God is . . . a tried and true help, a well-proven help. The verb *help* is used in verse 5: "God will help her right early." "At crack of dawn" is the more literal and far livelier translation of the Jerusalem Bible. We need not muddle through half the day, or half our lives, before God shows up, rubbing his eyes, asking if there is anything he might do for us.

He knows the kind of world we live in and our vulnerability to it, for he has taken up habitation in it himself (John 1:14). He anticipates our needs and plans ahead. He is there right on time to help, "at crack of dawn."

WHERE YOUR TREASURE IS

REMIND US OF GOD

"You shall be to Me a kingdom of priests."

EXODUS 19:6, NKJV

Embarrassingly forgetful of the God who saves us, and easily distracted from the God who is with us, we need priests to remind us of God, to confront us with God. And we need a lot of them. God, knowing our need, put us in a kingdom of priests. But for the most part they're priests who don't look like priests, priests who don't take on the airs of priests, priests who don't dress like priests, priests who don't talk like priests. But they're *priests* all the same.

LEAP OVER A WALL

THE GOSPEL PROMISE

*Our Lord Jesus Christ, . . . gave himself
for our sins to deliver us . . . according to
the will of our God and Father.*

GALATIANS 1:3–4, RSV

Any people who attempt to live in defiance of God—and every age makes the attempt—lives badly. Sin destroys our capacity to live. It weakens our vitality. It blinds us to truth. It incapacitates us for living out a healthy love and a vigorous peace. We need deliverance from it. God provides deliverance from it, decade after decade, generation after generation, "according to the will of our God and Father." That is the promise of the gospel.

TRAVELING LIGHT

ABSOLUTELY UNIQUE

Each of us is an original.

GALATIANS 5:26, THE MESSAGE

E ach of us is an absolutely unique combination of experience and intelligence and situation. The way we live out that uniqueness cannot be assigned by another, no matter how wise or authoritative. It must be creatively worked out in our own faith responses in the Spirit.

There are always some who know exactly what another is best suited for. But no one knows us well enough for that. Each of us has unique gifts, for which there are no precedents, yet which will be used in ministry. And we are quite free to resist anyone who tells us differently.

TRAVELING LIGHT

JOY AND PEACE

Do you see what this means—
all these pioneers who blazed the way. . . ? It means
we'd better get on with it . . . —and never quit!

HEBREWS 12:1, THE MESSAGE

My job as a pastor is not to solve people's problems or make them happy, but to help them see the grace operating in their lives. It's hard to do, because our whole culture is going the other direction, saying that if you're smart enough and get the right kind of help, you can solve all your problems. The truth is, there aren't very many happy people in the Bible. But there are people who are experiencing joy, peace, and the meaning of Christ's suffering in their lives.

THE CONTEMPLATIVE PASTOR

THE PRAYING COMMUNITY

Those who trust in GOD are like Zion Mountain:
nothing can move it.

PSALM 125:1, THE MESSAGE

All the psalms are prayers in community: people assembled, attentive before God, participating in a common posture, movement and speech, offering themselves and each other to their Lord. Prayer is not a private exercise, but a family convocation.

Prayer often originates when we are alone. Deep within us are "Sighs too deep for words." We pray our guilt, our hurt, our gaiety on the spot, not waiting until we can meet with a congregation or get into a church. All the same, for these prayers to develop into full maturity, they must be integrated into the praying community.

ANSWERING GOD

MAKING SENSE OF SUFFERING

Be agreeable, be sympathetic, be loving,
be compassionate, be humble.
That goes for all of you, no exceptions.

1 PETER 3:8, THE MESSAGE

T he biblical way to deal with suffering is to transform what is individual into something corporate.

Most cultures show a spontaneous comprehension of this. The suffering person is joined by friends who join their tears and prayers in a communal lament. They do not hush up the sound of weeping but augment it.

If others weep with me, there must be more to the suffering than my own petty weakness or selfish sense of loss. . . . The community votes with its tears that there is suffering that is worth weeping over.

FIVE SMOOTH STONES

UNCLUTTERED TIME

Work six days and do everything you need to do.
But the seventh day is a Sabbath to GOD, your God.

EXODUS 20:8, THE MESSAGE

S abbath: Uncluttered time and space to distance ourselves from the frenzy of our own activities so we can see what God has been and is doing. If we do not regularly quit work for one day a week we take ourselves far too seriously. The moral sweat pouring off our brows blinds us to the primal action of God in and around us.

Sabbath-keeping: Quieting the internal noise so we hear the still small voice of our Lord. Removing the distractions of pride so we discern the presence of Christ.

WORKING THE ANGLES

GOD IS NO BULLY

You're our living Father, our Redeemer,
famous from eternity!

ISAIAH 63:16, THE MESSAGE

How *does* God exercise his authority? Plainly, not with a heavy hand. He does not coerce. As one early church father put it, "Force is no attribute of God." God is not a bully. He is not a despot. He does not push His children around. He creates us, provides for us, loves us, and disciplines us; but He does not *make* us do anything. There are corrections and punishments, patient instruction and clear example, the disciplines of history and circumstance, but He does not force His will upon us.

LIKE DEW YOUR YOUTH

CALLED BY NAME

He calls his own sheep by name and leads them out.

JOHN 10:4, THE MESSAGE

At our birth we are named, not numbered. The name is part of speech by which we are recognized as a person. We are not classified as a species of animal. We are not labeled as a compound of chemicals. We are not assessed for our economical potential and given a cash value. We are named. . . .

Names mean something. A personal name designates what is irreducibly personal. . . .

The meaning of a name is not in the dictionary, not in the unconscious, not in the size of the lettering. It is in *relationship*—with God.

RUN WITH THE HORSES

OVERFLOWING BLESSING

My God shall supply all your need
according to His riches in glory by Christ Jesus.

PHILIPPIANS 4:19, NKJV

A wrong idea of reality leads to a wrong response to life. If we think God is stern and angry and despotic, we will live frightened. If we think that God is miserly and stingy, we will live feeling gypped. If we think that God is abstract and impersonal, we will live aimlessly and trivially.

The gospel teaches us that in every way God supplies—he overflows with blessing and salvation. In touch with that reality we live with a sense of abandonment and walk with a confident gaiety, freely trusting, freely hoping, freely loving.

TRAVELING LIGHT

SONGS OF VICTORY

GOD's strong name is our help,
the same GOD who made heaven and earth.

PSALM 124:8, THE MESSAGE

Faith develops out of the most difficult aspects of our existence, not the easiest.

We speak our words of praise in a world that is hellish; we sing our songs of victory in a world where things get messy; we live our joy among people who neither understand nor encourage us. But the content of our lives is God, not humanity. We are not scavenging in the dark alleys of the world, poking in its garbage cans for a bare subsistence. We are traveling in the light, toward God who is rich in mercy and strong to save. It is Christ, not culture, that defines our lives. It is the help we experience, not the hazards we risk that shapes our days.

A LONG OBEDIENCE

PATTERNS FOR LIFE

Take a long, loving look at me,
your High God, above politics, above everything.

PSALM 46:10, THE MESSAGE

Civilization is littered with unsolved problems, baffling impasses. The best minds of the world are at the end of their tether. . . . The most relevant contribution that Christians make at these points of impasse is the act of prayer—determined, repeated, leisurely meetings with a personal and living God.

Prayer is not all we do. Patterns and behaviors develop out of the prayers. There is also child raising, lawn mowing, and making a living. There is intelligence to be exercised, behavior to be shaped, moral decisions and responsible courage.

WHERE YOUR TREASURE IS

GOD'S GLORY

"I will not put forth my hand against my lord;
for he is the LORD's anointed."

1 SAMUEL 24:10, RSV

David penetrated Saul's camp in the middle of the night and came upon Saul fast asleep and unprotected. He could easily have killed him but didn't. David's wilderness-trained eyes looked on Saul and saw not Saul the enemy but the Saul the God-anointed. In the solitude and silence and emptiness of the wilderness, uncluttered and undistracted by what everyone else was saying and doing, David was able to see God's glory where no one else could see it—in Saul. . . .

Through wilderness-testing David learned to see God in places and things he would never have thought to look previously.

LEAP OVER A WALL

LIVING LARGE

*I'll make a list of GOD's gracious dealings,
all the things GOD has done that need praising.*

ISAIAH 63:7, THE MESSAGE

There are tendencies within us and forces outside us that relentlessly reduce God to a checklist of explanations, or a handbook of moral precepts, or an economic arrangement, or a political expediency, or a pleasure boat. God is reduced to what can be measured, used, weighed, gathered, controlled, or felt. Insofar as we accept these reductionist explanations, our lives become bored, depressed, or mean. We live stunted like acorns in a terrarium. But oak trees need soil, sun, rain, and wind.

REVERSED THUNDER

DENY YOURSELF

"If any want to become my followers, let them deny themselves and take up their cross and follow me."

MARK 8:34, NRSV

In the first half of Saint Mark's Gospel . . . Jesus is primarily presented as doing things for us, telling us the way things are. He helps and heals, he directs and teaches. He is in the process of revealing God to us by restoring all things, making all things new. . . . It is at this point, but not a moment before, that Jesus introduces his . . . call for renunciation: deny yourself; take up your cross daily.

Note well: this is not a prohibition to be obeyed; it is a renunciation to be embraced. He does not chain the disciples up and march them to Jerusalem and the cross. He invites them to *follow* him in the renunciation that he embraces on the road to resurrection.

LIKE DEW YOUR YOUTH

FAITH LASTS

"Father, forgive them;
they don't know what they're doing."

LUKE 23:34, THE MESSAGE

F aith lasts. We remember the way it was with
Jesus. Has anyone ever experienced such a
relentless, merciless pounding from within and from
without? First there were the cunning attempts to
get him off track, every temptation disguised as a
suggestion for improvement. . . . Then, at the other
end, when all the temptations had failed, that
brutal assault when his body was turned into a
torture chamber. And we know the result: an
incomprehensible kindness ("Father, forgive them"),
an unprecedented serenity ("Father, into your hands
I commit my spirit") and—resurrection.

The way of faith is not a fad that is taken up
in one century only to be discarded in the next. It
lasts. It is a way that works.

A LONG OBEDIENCE

GOD'S THEATER

The mountains take one look at GOD
and melt, melt like wax before earth's Lord.

PSALM 97:5, THE MESSAGE

Creation is our place for meeting God and conversing with him. . . . We take box seats in this creation theater when we pray. We look around. The mountains are huge, heaving their bulk upwards. The creeks spill across the rocks, giving extravagant light shows under the hemlocks. . . .

The psalmists have season tickets in this theater. . . . They pray breathless in awe, laughing and crying, puzzled and dismayed, complaining and believing. . . . All is not to their liking, and during some scenes they seem about to walk out. But they do not.

They don't walk out because their business is prayer, and there is no prayer, real prayer, outside the theater.

ANSWERING GOD

LIVING BY TRUTH

*God wants us to grow up, to know the whole truth
and tell it in love—like Christ in everything.*

EPHESIANS 4:15, THE MESSAGE

We must learn to live by the truth, not by our feelings, not by the world's opinion, not by what the latest statistical survey tells us is the accepted morality, not by what advertisers tell us is the most gratifying lifestyle. We are trained in the biblical faith to take lightly what experts say, the pollsters say, the politicians say, the pastors say. We are trained to listen to the Word of God, to test everything against what God reveals to us in Christ, to discover all meaning and worth by examining life in relation to God's will.

RUN WITH THE HORSES

OUR CUSTODIAN

The law was our custodian until Christ came.

GALATIANS 3:24, RSV

The meaning of the Greek word *paidagogos* that lies behind the English word *custodian* often loses something in translation. Greek families that were well enough off to have slaves chose one of them, usually an old and trusted slave, to be in charge of their child or children from the ages of six to sixteen. This custodian went with the child to school to see that no harm or mischief came to him. He was not the schoolmaster. He had nothing to do with the actual teaching of the child. It was only his duty to take him safely to the school and deliver him to the teacher. That, says Paul, is how the law works: it delivers us to the place of faith, to Christ.

TRAVELING LIGHT

GIVING UP MY WILL

Go after a life of love as if
your life depended on it—because it does.

1 CORINTHIANS 14:1, THE MESSAGE

L ove is defined by a willingness to give up my
  will . . . , a voluntary crucifixion.

[In marriage] we find ourselves in daily
relationship with a complex reality we did not
make, . . . with a will, the freedom to choose and
direct and intend a shared life intimacy. . . .

We learn soon that love does not develop when
we impose our will on the other, but only when we
enter into sensitive responsiveness to the will of the
other. . . . If the operation is mutual, which it
sometimes is, a great love is the consequence.

THE CONTEMPLATIVE PASTOR

GOD—PERSONAL AND PRESENT

GOD is bedrock under my feet,
the castle in which I live.

PSALM 18:2, THE MESSAGE

David believed in God, thought about God, imagined God, addressed God, prayed to God. The largest part of David's existence wasn't David but God. . . .

David was immersed in God. Every visibility revealed for him an invisibility. David named God by metaphor. . . .

Nothing in or about God was left on the shelf to be considered at a later time or to be brought up for discussion when there was leisure for it. God was personal and present and required *response;* "I love you . . . I live in you . . . I run for dear life to you."

LEAP OVER A WALL

PULLED INTO COMMUNITY

My mouth's full of great praise for GOD,
I'm singing his hallelujahs surrounded by crowds.

PSALM 109:30, THE MESSAGE

The gospel pulls us into community. One of the immediate changes that the gospel makes is grammatical: we instead of I, our instead of my, us instead of me. . . .

A believing community is the context for the life of faith. Love cannot exist in isolation: away from others, love bloats into pride. Grace cannot be received privately: cut off from others it is perverted into greed. Hope cannot develop in solitude: separated from the community, it goes to seed in the form of fantasies. No gift, no virtue can develop and remain healthy apart from the community of faith.

REVERSED THUNDER

CONTAGIOUS FAITH

GOD's business is putting things right;
he loves getting the lines straight, setting us straight.

PSALM 11:7, THE MESSAGE

The Hebrews were not an aggressively proselytizing people, but they were an intensely serious people—serious about the meaning of life, serious about covenant with God. They did not campaign to convert others to their way of life, but their faith was contagious. The peoples among whom they lived were attracted by the dazzling intensities of their worship and were drawn into the maturing pilgrimage of holiness. . . . They discovered, through the witness of the Jew, the reality of God who created, who entered into suffering, who carved out a way of redemption.

WHERE YOUR TREASURE IS

THE PEOPLE GOD GIVES

*You were all called to travel on the same road
and in the same direction,
so stay together, both outwardly and inwardly.*

EPHESIANS 4:4, THE MESSAGE

Most disappointments in the church are because of failed expectations. We expect a disciplined army of committed men and women who courageously lay siege to the worldly powers; instead we find some people who are more concerned with getting rid of the crabgrass in their lawns. We expect a community of saints who are mature in the virtues of love and mercy, and find ourselves working on a church supper where there is more gossip than there are casseroles. . . .

At such times it is more important to examine and change our expectations than to change the church, for the church is not what we organize but what God gives, not the people we want to be with but the people God gives us to be with.

REVERSED THUNDER

COURAGEOUS PRAYER

No god is great like God!
You're the God who makes things happen.

PSALM 77:13–14, THE MESSAGE

If we think that prayer is going to get us out of the conflict, we are misinformed. If we think that an immersion in the Psalms will insulate us from the abrasive news of the day, we are mistaken. If we think that looking to God fills us with undisturbed peace and unalloyed joy so that there is simply no space left in our lives for an awareness of barbarity, we are wrong. Nature is violent. Governments are violent. People are violent. Reading the Psalms is a shocking experience. Praying is a courageous act.

WHERE YOUR TREASURE IS

GOD GIVES HIMSELF

He gave the poor a safe place to live,
treated their clans like well-cared-for sheep.

PSALM 107:41, THE MESSAGE

There is a very close relation in Hebrew between the words *poor* (*'aniyyim*) and *humble* (*'anawim*). *Poor* designates a socioeconomic state; *humble*, a moral-spiritual condition. What they have in common is nonpossesiveness. Whether by circumstance or by choice these people are not in control. Their either cannot or do not hold the reins of their destiny. Because they are out of control, they are able to respond to and receive the gifts of God's sovereign bounty. . . .

In a life characterized by God giving himself and blessing us, we begin by not having.

WHERE YOUR TREASURE IS

LIVING FREE

Christ has set us free to live a free life. . . . Never again let anyone put a harness of slavery on you.

GALATIANS 5:1, THE MESSAGE

One day [the Hebrews] were a demoralized and unarmed people crushed under the cruelty and whim of an enslaving religion; the next day they were victoriously free, singing the praises of a redeeming God. They left their slave life behind them. They also left, it turned out, a comfortable security, a sophisticated culture, . . . and a dependable routine. In the desert wastes they were absolutely dependent on a God whom they could not see. . . .

Here they would be trained in living as free people and not as slaves, discover what it means to live by faith and not by works, realize what it means to live under the provident blessing of God and not under the tyranny of a pharaoh.

TRAVELING LIGHT

PRAYING THE PAIN

*Help, GOD—the bottom has fallen
out of my life! Master, hear my cry for help!*

PSALM 130:1, THE MESSAGE

A Christian is a person who decides to face and live through suffering. So we find in Psalm 130 not so much as a trace of those things that are so common among us, which rob us of our humanity when we suffer and make the pain so much more terrible to bear. No glib smart answers. No lectures on our misfortunes. . . . No hasty Band-Aid treatments covering up our trouble so the rest of society doesn't have to look at it.

None of that: the suffering is held up and proclaimed—and prayed.

A Long Obedience

OCTOBER

God gives lavishly.

PRAYER IS PRACTICAL

He attends to the prayer of the wretched.
He won't dismiss their prayer.

PSALM 102:16, THE MESSAGE

Prayer orients us to God's design.

Out of the silence of heaven, actions are prepared. The prayers are not simply stored on the altar, they are mixed with the fire of God's spirit and returned to earth. Prayer is as much outer as inner. It is the most practical thing anyone can do. It is not mystical escape, it is historical engagement. Prayer participates in God's action. God gathers our cries and our praises, our petitions and intercessions, and uses them. The prayers that ascended to God now descend to earth.

REVERSED THUNDER

THE MIDDLE OF THE STORY

I . . . join hands with others . . . , singing God-songs
at the top of my lungs, telling God-stories.

PSALM 26:8, THE MESSAGE

We enter a world we didn't create. We grow into a life already provided for us. We arrive in a complex of relationships with other wills and destinies that are already in full operation before we are introduced. If we are going to live appropriately, we must be aware that we are living in the middle of a story that was begun and will be concluded by another. And this other is God.

RUN WITH THE HORSES

REPENTANCE

"Repent, for the kingdom of heaven is at hand!"

MATTHEW 3:2, NKJV

Repentance is not an emotion. It is not feeling sorry for your sins. It is a decision. It is deciding that you have been wrong in supposing that you could manage your own life and be your own god. It is deciding that you were wrong in thinking that you had, or could get, the strength, education and training to make it on your own. It is deciding that you have been told a pack of lies about yourself and your neighbors and your world.

And it is deciding that God in Jesus Christ is telling you the truth. . . . Repentance is a decision to follow Jesus Christ and become his pilgrim in the path of peace.

A LONG OBEDIENCE

GOD BRINGS HELP

God is our refuge and strength,
a very present help in trouble.

PSALM 46:1, RSV

To the objection "I prayed and cried out for help, but no help came," the answer is "But it did. The help was there. It was right at hand. You were looking for something quite different, perhaps, but God brought the help that would change your life into health, into wholeness for eternity. . . ."

Instead of asking why the help has not come, the person at prayer learns to look carefully at what is actually going on in his or her life, . . . and ask, "Could this be the help he is providing? I never thought of *this* in terms of help, but maybe it is."

WHERE YOUR TREASURE IS

THE CENTER OF LIFE

We received both the generous gift of his life and
the urgent task of passing it on to others who receive
it by entering into obedient trust in Jesus.

ROMANS 1:5, THE MESSAGE

Paul submitted himself to the will of God and agreed to let God work in him; at the same time he quit trying to subject other people to his will, forcing them to fit into what he thought was best for them.

That is the heart of the Christian story. We accept Christ as Lord and Savior. We realize that God is the living center of life and that he has provided the means by which we can live in conscious, glad relationship with him. We live not by moral projects but by obedient faith.

TRAVELING LIGHT

PRAYER IN CONGREGATION

Confess your sins to each other and pray for each other so that you can live together whole and healed.

JAMES 5:16, THE MESSAGE

The congregation is a place where I'm gradually learning that prayer is not conditioned or authenticated by my feelings. Nothing is more devastating to prayer than when I begin to evaluate prayer by my feelings, and think that in order to pray I have to have a certain sense, a certain spiritual attentiveness or peace or, on the other side, anguish.

That's virtually impossible to learn by yourself. But if I'm in a congregation, I learn over and over again that prayer will go on whether I feel like it or not, or even if I sleep through the whole thing.

THE CONTEMPLATIVE PASTOR

ETERNALLY IMPORTANT

Gracious speech is like clover honey—
good taste to the soul, quick energy for the body.

PROVERBS 16:24, THE MESSAGE

Our daily encounters with bank tellers, post office clerks, and gas station attendants are, each one, elements of sin and grace. All of these people and each of these encounters is a significant detail in the life of faith. But we are not aware of it. Most of the time we are not living in a crisis in which we are conscious of our need of God, yet everything we do is critical, to our faith, and God is critically involved in it.

All day long we are doing eternally important things without knowing it. All through the day we inadvertently speak words that enter people lives and change them in minor or major ways, and we never know it.

REVERSED THUNDER

WORDS SPOKEN

The message you are hearing isn't mine.
It's the message of the Father who sent me.

JOHN 14:24, THE MESSAGE

One large dimension of St. John's Gospel shows Jesus bringing men and women into consversation with God—no longer merely reading the Scriptures, at which many of them were quite adept, but *listening* to God, which they hardly guessed was possible. This succession of conversation was closely followed and believingly entered into—Mary at Cana, Nicodemus at Night, the Samaritan woman, the Bethzatha paralytic. . . .

At no place in St. John's Gospel is the word of God simply there—carved in stone, painted on a sign, printed in a book. The word is always *sound:* words spoken and heard.

WORKING THE ANGLES

WHAT IS WRONG?

Don't use your anger as fuel for revenge.
And don't stay angry.

EPHESIANS 4:26, THE MESSAGE

Anger is most useful as a diagnostic tool. When anger erupts in us, it is a signal that something is wrong. Something isn't working right. There is evil or incompetence or stupidity lurking about. Anger is our sixth sense for sniffing out wrong in the neighborhood.

What anger fails to do, though, is tell us whether the wrong is outside or inside us. We usually begin by assuming that the wrong is outside us—our spouse or our child or God has done something wrong, and we are angry. But when we track the anger carefully, we often find it leads to a wrong within us—wrong information, inadequate understanding, underdeveloped heart.

UNDER THE UNPREDICTABLE PLANT

DOING THE JOB WELL

Keep your eye on what you're doing;
. . . do a thorough job as God's servant.

2 TIMOTHY 4:5, THE MESSAGE

Many people . . . spend their working days "making a living" and their weekends and evenings trying to make up for the lack of meaning in their jobs by doing "Christian work." But that doesn't have to happen. Almost any job can be used to channel discipleship. In every decade Christians have been engaged in hundreds of occupations at all levels of society, each doing the job well "unto the Lord." And disciples have been made—who knows how many?

LIKE DEW YOUR YOUTH

LINKED WITH GOD

You shaped me first inside, then out;
you formed me in my mother's womb.

PSALM 139:13, THE MESSAGE

On the day their son was born, Hilkiah and his wife named him in anticipation of the way God would act in his life. In hope they saw the years unfolding and their son as one in whom the Lord would be lifted up: *Jeremiah*—the Lord is exalted.

Jeremiah—a name linked with the name and action of God. The only thing more significant to Jeremiah than his own being was God's being. He fought in the name of the Lord and explored the reality of God and in the process grew and developed, ripened and matured. He was always reaching out, always finding more truth, getting in touch with more of God, becoming more himself, more human.

RUN WITH THE HORSES

WISDOM

The wise accumulate wisdom.

PROVERBS 14:24, THE MESSAGE

The opposite of *foolish* in Scripture is *wise*. Wise refers to skill in living. It does not mean, primarily, the person who knows the right answers to things, but one who has developed the right responses (relationships) to persons, to God.

The wise understand how the world works, know about patience and love, listening and grace, adoration and beauty; know that other people are awesome creatures to be respected and befriended, especially the ones that I cannot get anything out of; . . . know that God is an ever-present center, . . . an all-encompassing love.

WHERE YOUR TREASURE IS

THE CHRISTIAN LIFE

*Your life is a journey you must
travel with a deep consciousness of God.*

1 PETER 1:17, THE MESSAGE

The recurrent error of our technologically conditioned age is to look for what's wrong in our lives so that we can fix it, or what need's doing so that we can have something worthwhile to do. There *are* things wrong that need fixing; and there *are* things that need doing. But the Christian life starts at the other end—not with us but with God: What is God doing that I can respond to? How is God expressing his love and grace so that I can live appreciatively and in obedience?

LEAP OVER A WALL

FROM THE CENTER

The prayer of a person living right with God is
something powerful to be reckoned with.

JAMES 5:17, THE MESSAGE

When we take our place in a worshiping congregation we are not in charge. Someone else has built the place of prayer, someone else has established the time for prayer, someone else tells us to begin to pray. All of this takes place in a context in which the word of God is primary: God's word audible in Scripture and sermon, God's word visible in baptism and eucharist.

This is the center in which we learn to pray. We do not, of course, remain in this center. Lines of praying radiate and lead us outwards. From this center we go to our closets or the mountains, into the streets and the markets, and continue our praying. But it is essential to understand that the prayer goes from the center *outwards*.

ANSWERING GOD

GOD IS STEADFAST

Blessed is GOD, Israel's God, always, always, always.

PSALM 41:13, THE MESSAGE

Israel was up one day and down the next. One day they were marching in triumph through the Red Sea, singing songs of victory, the next day they were grumbling in the desert because they missed having Egyptian steak and potatoes for supper. One day they were marching around Jericho blowing trumpets and raising hearty hymns, and the next they were plunged into an orgy at some Canaanite fertility shrine. . . .

But all the time, as we read that saw-toothed history, we realize something solid and steady: they are always God's people. God is steadfastly with them, in mercy and judgement, insistently gracious.

A LONG OBEDIENCE

KING AND SLAVE

Christ Jesus came into the world to save sinners.

1 TIMOTHY 1:15, RSV

When Jesus designated himself Son of Man, which he did frequently, it could only have evoked puzzled consternation. . . . His use of the title aroused expectations of redemption; his refusal to call down legions of angels to establish his power dashed the expectations. Yet he continued to insist on the title.

It is difficult to [imagine] the incongruity . . . when this Son of Man has dinner with a prostitute, stops for lunch with a tax-collector, wastes time blessing children when there were Roman legions to be chased from the land, heals unimportant losers and ignores high-achieving Pharisees and influential Sadducees. Jesus juxtaposed the most glorious title available to him with the most menial of life-styles in the culture. He talked like a king and acted like a slave.

REVERSED THUNDER

PERSEVERANCE

*I am the Good Shepherd. The Good Shepherd puts
the sheep before himself, sacrifices himself if necessary.*

JOHN 10:11, THE MESSAGE

Christian discipleship is a process of paying
more and more attention to God's
righteousness and less and less attention to our
own. It is finding the meaning of our lives not by
probing our moods and motives and morals but by
believing in God's will and purposes. It is making
a map of the faithfulness of God, not charting the
rise and fall of our enthusiasms. It is out of such a
reality that we acquire perseverance.

A LONG OBEDIENCE

LOOKING FOR BARGAINS

You have one Master, one faith, one baptism,
one God and Father of all, who rules over all, works
through all, and is present in all. Everything you are
and think and do is permeated with Oneness.

EPHESIANS 4:5–6, THE MESSAGE

Why do we find it so difficult to accept the truth? Because we are looking for bargains. We want shortcuts. There are no easy ways. There is only one way. If we are going to be complete human beings, we are going to have to do it with God. We will have to be rescued from these despotic egos. . . . We will have to expose the life of self-centeredness and proclaim the truth of God-centeredness.

RUN WITH THE HORSES

FREE TO TRUST

Now we, brethren, like Isaac, are children of promise.

GALATIANS 4:28, RSV

One son was born because God promised, the other son was born because Abraham doubted. Ishmael was a product of human impatience, the human trying to do God's work for him; Isaac was the result of God doing his own work in his own time. Ishmael caused nothing but trouble; Isaac continued in the faithful covenant of the freely living God. The great disaster of Abraham's life was that he used Hagar to get what he thought God wanted for him. The great achievement of his life was that God did for him apart from any programs or plans that he put into action. . . .

Because God freely keeps his promises, we are free to trust.

TRAVELING LIGHT

A CELEBRATION

Every time you eat this bread and every time
you drink this cup, you reenact in your words and
actions the death of the Master.

1 CORINTHIANS 11:26, THE MESSAGE

Eucharist is at one and the same time ordinary
and extraordinary. . . . Meals, in all cultures,
seem to have this capability of stretching from the
ordinary to the extraordinary and interpenetrating
them. The three meals of our ordinary days are
routine. But when we want to celebrate a great
occasion, wedding or birthday or anniversary, we do
not find it unnatural to use the meal as the means
for expressing intensity, ecstasy, and consummation.

Salvation, on the one hand, is Christ on the
cross and risen from the tomb; on the other hand, it
is eating bread and drinking wine. In the eucharistic
meal, these cannot be separated: salvation is both
Christ on Golgotha and Christ in me.

REVERSED THUNDER

KINGDOM CITIZENS

His love has taken over our lives;
God's faithful ways are eternal.

PSALM 117:2, THE MESSAGE

God does not save us so that we can cultivate private ecstasies. He does not save us so that we can be guaranteed a reservation in a heavenly mansion. We are made citizens in a kingdom, that is, a society.

He teaches us the language of the kingdom by providing the psalms, which turn out to be as concerned with rough-and-tumble politics as they are with quiet waters of piety. So why do we easily imagine God tenderly watching over a falling sparrow but boggle at believing that he is present in the hugger-mugger of smoke-filled rooms?

WHERE YOUR TREASURE IS

HAZARDS OF FAITH

*It's what we trust in but don't yet
see that keeps us going.*

2 CORINTHIANS 5:7, THE MESSAGE

Flannery O'Connor once remarked that she had an aunt who thought that nothing happened in a story unless somebody got married or shot at the end of it. But life seldom provides such definitive endings. As a consequence, the best stories, the stories that show us true condition by immersing us in reality, don't provide them either.

Life is ambiguous. There are loose ends. It takes maturity to live with the ambiguity and the chaos, the absurdity and the untidiness. If we refuse to live with it, we exclude something, and what we exclude may very well be essential and dear—the hazards of faith, the mysteries of God.

RUN WITH THE HORSES

WEAKNESS AND STRENGTH

*Regarding life together and getting
along with each other . . . just love one another!*

1 THESSALONIANS 4:9, THE MESSAGE

Compassionate, generous, spontaneous mutuality develops when we realize two things: there is no even distribution of strengths. The curses and the blessings are unevenly distributed. Some have heavier loads put on them than others—burdens of illness, work, family, emotional trauma. . . . And not all of us get equal strengths. Some of us are born with strong bodies and fragile emotions, others with robust emotions and weak bodies.

Once we understand this, we will not arrogantly separate ourselves from others when we find ourselves strong, nor will we withdraw in groveling self-pity when we find ourselves weak. The Christian is free to share both weakness and strength, burdens and abilities.

TRAVELING LIGHT

CHILDLIKE TRUST

Unless you accept God's kingdom
in the simplicity of a child, you'll never get in.

MARK 10:15, THE MESSAGE

Christian faith is not neurotic dependency but childlike trust. . . .We do not cling to God desperately out of fear and the panic of insecurity. We come to him freely in faith and love.

Our Lord gave us the picture of the child as a model for Christian faith not because of the child's helplessness but because of the child's willingness to be led, to be taught, to be blessed.

A LONG OBEDIENCE

A GOD-AFFIRMING LIFE

God's chosen is beloved. I mean
David and all his children—always.

PSALM 18:51, THE MESSAGE

David's . . . was a God-affirming and God affirmed life, large and expansive—what Jesus named "more and better life than they ever dreamed of" (John 10:10). . . .

David with all his rough edges. He never got around to loving his enemies the way his descendant Jesus would do it; his morals and manners left a lot to be desired. These aren't narrated as blemishes, however, but as conditions that we share. They aren't narrated to legitimize bad behavior but are set down as proof that we don't first become good and then get God. First we get God—and then, over a patient lifetime, we're trained in God's ways.

LEAP OVER A WALL

CHRIST IN THE MIDST

In the midst of the lampstands
I saw one like the Son of Man.

REVELATION 1:13, NRSV

When St. John turned towards the trumpet voice . . . the first thing he saw was seven gold lampstands, "which are the seven churches" to which he was pastor. Then, in their midst, he saw the one "like a Son of Man" who was Jesus, the Christ.

It is not possible to have Christ apart from the church. We try. We would very much like to have Christ apart from the contradictions and distractions of the other persons who believe in him, or say that they do. We want a Christ who is pure goodness, beauty, and truth. We prefer to worship him under the soaring symphony, or by means of a penetrating poetry. . . .

But to all this aspiring aestheticism the gospel says No.

REVERSED THUNDER

GOD RULES NOW

Thy decrees are very sure; holiness befits thy house,
O LORD, for evermore.

PSALM 93:5, RSV

O LORD, *for evermore* . . . affirms the rule in ordinary time. "As the days stretch out through history" catches the tone of the Hebrew "forever," *l'orek yamiim.* This is not God's rule eternal in the heavens apart from human history but God's rule working itself out through the calendar.

Prayer is not a patient wait for the rule to come into effect at the end of history, it is a patient participation in present rule. God's rule is not being held in reserve to be inaugurated at some future date, after centuries of human rulers have their best (or worst). It is in operation now.

WHERE YOUR TREASURE IS

GOD IS HOLY

GOD is higher than anything and anyone,
outshining everything you can see in the skies.

PSALM 113:4, THE MESSAGE

oly is a word that we use to designate the otherness, the purity, the beauty of God. *God* is holy. . . .God isn't a human being, even the best of human beings, writ large. Because God is *other,* God is therefore also mystery. . . . God is so *other* that we can never pretend to predict what God will do, or get God under control in any way whatever. Our only appropriate approach to God is in awe and reverence, in humble and submissive worship.

LEAP OVER A WALL

ADMIRED VIRTUE

The payoff for meekness and Fear-of-GOD is
plenty and honor and a satisfying life.

PROVERBS 22:4, THE MESSAGE

Humility (which is the old name for unself-assertion) is probably the least sought-after virtue in America. Mostly, it is despised. At best it is treated with condescension, which is perhaps permissible among the timorous devout who have no aptitude for the affairs of this world. But for centuries, humility was the most admired, if not the most practiced, of the virtues. Can so many whom the world has counted wise be wrong?

WHERE YOUR TREASURE IS

THE LANGUAGE OF PRAYER

O LORD, how many are my foes!

PSALM 3:1, RSV

"O LORD, how many are my foes!" Brief, urgent, frightened words—a person in trouble, crying out to God for help. The language is personal, direct, desperate. This is the language of prayer: men and women calling out their trouble—pain, guilt, doubt, despair—to God. . . .

The language of prayer is forged in the crucible of trouble. When we can't help ourselves and call for help, when we don't like where we are and want out, when we don't like who we are and want a change, we use primal language, and this language becomes the root language of prayer.

ANSWERING GOD

LIVING LIFE WELL

Help me understand these things inside
and out so I can ponder your miracle-wonders.

PSALM 119:27, THE MESSAGE

What do Bible stories tell us about living this human life well, living it totally? Primarily and mostly they tell us that it means dealing with God. It means dealing with a lot of other things as well: danger and parents and enemies and friends and lovers and children and wives and pride and humiliation and . . . sickness and death and sexuality . . . and fear and peace—to say nothing of diapers . . . and breakfast and traffic jams and clogged drainpipes and bounced checks. But always, at the forefront and in the background of circumstances, events, and people, it's God.

LEAP OVER A WALL

NOVEMBER

We live in response
to the living God.

GOD'S WONDERFUL WORKS

Come, behold the works of the LORD.

PSALM 46:8, RSV

Everybody else is noisier than God. The headlines and neon lights and amplifying systems of the world announce human works. But what of God's works? They are unadvertised but also inescapable, if we simply look. They are everywhere. They are marvelous. But God has no public relations agency. He mounts no publicity campaign to get our attention. He simply invites us to look. Prayer is looking at the works of the Lord.

WHERE YOUR TREASURE IS

COMMISSIONED BY GOD

*I have suffered the loss of all things, and I regard
them as rubbish, in order that I may gain Christ.*

PHILIPPIANS 3:8, NRSV

"Paul, an apostle . . ."An apostle is a person
invited by Christ to be with him and then sent
out to represent his gospel. . . . That is Paul's
identity. Everything he did and spoke and wrote
was a result of being with Christ and being sent
out by Christ. . . . He had nothing of his own to
say, no good works of his own to practice. He was
an authorized and commissioned representative of
his Lord.

Kierkegaard once distinguished between a
genius and an apostle by saying that the genius
impresses us with his own brilliance, the apostle
with God's glory.

TRAVELING LIGHT

THE CENTER OF PRAYER

*Carefully build yourselves up in this most
holy faith by praying in the Holy Spirit, staying
right at the center of God's love.*

JUDE 20, THE MESSAGE

I f somebody comes to me and says, "Teach me
how to pray," I say, "Be at this church at nine
o'clock on Sunday morning." That's where you
learn how to pray. . . .

Prayer has to be a response to what God has
said. The worshiping congregation—hearing the
Word read and preached, and celebrating it in the
sacraments—is the place where I learn how to pray
and where I practice prayer. It is a center from
which I pray. From it I go to my closet or to the
mountains and continue to pray.

THE CONTEMPLATIVE PASTOR

GOD'S WAYS

Salvation now, GOD.
Salvation now! Oh yes, GOD—a free and full life.

PSALM 118:25, THE MESSAGE

While David knelt at the brook, the world was bounded on one side by an arrogant and bullying people of Philistia and on the other by the demoralized and anxious people of Israel. To the north of the brook the powerful but stupid giant; to the south of the brook the anointed but deeply flawed king. No one could have guessed that the young man picking stones out of the brook was doing the most significant work of the day. . . .

David kneeling, unhurried and calm, opened up another option: God, God's ways, God's salvation.

LEAP OVER A WALL

NEW EVERY MORNING

Great is your faithfulness! Yahweh is
my portion, I tell myself, therefore I will hope.

LAMENTATIONS 3:19–24, RSV

The great phrase here is "Yahweh is my portion," a quote from the Torah. Centuries earlier the Lord had said it, and Levi had accepted it (Deut. 10:9; Num. 18:20). . . . The ancient phrase had been handed down through generations, held onto tenaciously through the worst of troubles.

The people knew there was a communion with a merciful God that could not be lost because it could not be touched by the dislocations of external circumstance. The chaos and darkness of suffering become first-day light. "Yahweh's mercy is surely not at an end, nor is his pity exhausted. It is new every morning. Great is your faithfulness!"

FIVE SMOOTH STONES

WORSHIP IS ESSENTIAL

Come, let's shout praises to GOD,
raise the roof for the Rock who saved us!

PSALM 95:1, THE MESSAGE

Worship is the essential and central act of the Christian. We do many other things in preparation for and as a result of worship: sing, write, witness, heal, teach, paint, serve, help, build, clean, smile. But the centering act is worship.

Worship is the act of giving committed attention to the being and action of God. The Christian life is posited on the faith that God is in action. When we worship, it doesn't look like we are doing much—and we aren't. We are looking at what God is doing and orienting our action to the compass points of creation and covenant, judgement and salvation.

Nothing that we do has more effect in heaven or on earth.

REVERSED THUNDER

ALL IS GOD'S

Every detail in our lives of love
for God is worked into something good.

ROMANS 8:28, THE MESSAGE

God has had plans for us from before our birth. He has never been apart from us. That which took place in the years before our acceptance of Christ's love is not rejected but used. Nothing is wasted in the free life of faith. Now all is God's. . . . The change penetrates every part of our selves and our history, not just the "spiritual" parts, not just the good parts. The inferiorities we feel, the inadequacies we sense, the sins we regret, the differences that make us feel like outsiders—these are all . . . transformed into Christ-affirmed features that express the power and glory of God.

TRAVELING LIGHT

WE LISTEN

What you say goes, GOD, and stays, as permanent
as the heavens. Your truth never goes out of fashion.

PSALM 119:89–90, THE MESSAGE

The intent in reading Scripture, among people of faith, is to extend the range of our listening to the God who reveals himself in word, to become acquainted with the ways in which he has spoken in various times and places, along with the ways in which people respond when he speaks.

The Christian conviction is that God speaks reality into being—creation into shape, salvation into action. It is also a Christian conviction that *we* are *that* which is spoken into a creation shape and a salvation action. We are what happens when the word is spoken. So we listen in order to find out what is going on—in *us*.

WORKING THE ANGLES

A HUNGER FOR GOD

Is anyone crying for help?
God is listening, ready to rescue you.

PSALM 34:17, THE MESSAGE

All men and women hunger for God. The hunger is masked and misinterpreted in many ways, but it is always there. Everyone is on the verge of crying out "My Lord and my God!" but the cry is drowned out by doubt or defiance, muffled by the dull ache of their routines, masked by their cozy accommodations with mediocrity.

Then something happens—a word, an event, a dream—and there is a push toward awareness of an incredible Grace, a dazzling Desire, a defiant Hope, a courageous Faithfulness.

UNDER THE UNPREDICTABLE PLANT

A LIFE OF WITNESS

God takes particular pleasure
in acts of worship . . . that take place in kitchen
and workplace and on the streets.

HEBREWS 13:16, THE MESSAGE

We tend, in our society, to exalt work as such. The Bible doesn't do that. We place a high valuation on a person who works at a good job. We pay that person a lot of money and respect. But Jesus was a carpenter and Paul was a tentmaker. Neither job was exceptional in its demands, its prestige, or its usefulness to humankind. Both jobs, though (and there are numerous other biblical examples), became the working context for a life of witness. They used work as a context in which to obey the Great Commission.

LIKE DEW YOUR YOUTH

LIVING IN THE OPEN

My ego is no longer central. . . . I am
no longer driven to impress God. Christ lives in me.

GALATIANS 2:20, THE MESSAGE

Living in the open means that we don't have to hide who we really are, whitewash our reputations, or disguise our hearts. We can be open about who we are, about what we have thought and felt and done. We don't have to exhaust ourselves to project the blame for who we are on God on our parents or on society. We don't have to make up fancy excuses.

How refreshing that is! People who are always blaming others for the difficulties they experience in life . . . are incapacitated for living freely. . . . But accepting ourselves just as we are puts us in touch with who we really are and discovers large tracts of responsibility in which we can experience forgiveness and . . . relationship with God.

TRAVELING LIGHT

GOD AT OUR SIDE

God is a safe place to hide,
ready to help when we need him.

PSALM 46:1, THE MESSAGE

People of faith have the same needs for protection and security as anyone else. We are no better than others in that regard. What is different is that we find that we don't have to build our own: "God is a safe place to hide, ready to help when we need him."

We don't always have to be looking over our shoulder lest evil overtake us unawares. We don't always have to keep our eyes on our footsteps lest we slip, inadvertently, on a temptation. God is at our side.

A LONG OBEDIENCE

DIVINE WORK

*GOD took the Man and set him
down in the Garden of Eden to work the
ground and keep it in order.*

GENESIS 2:15, THE MESSAGE

The test of our work is not the profit we gain
from it or the status we receive from it but
its effects in creation. Are persons impoverished?
Is the land diminished? Is society defrauded? Is the
world less or more because of my work? . . .

No work can be reduced to what we do for a
living. All work is participation in the divine work.
God works and therefore we work.

WHERE YOUR TREASURE IS

A LIFE OF BELIEF

*Everything that goes into a life
of pleasing God has been miraculously given
to us by getting to know, personally
and intimately, the One who invited us to God.*

2 PETER 1:3, THE MESSAGE

The Christian life isn't monitored and regulated by a religious bureaucracy. God the Father, Son, and Holy Ghost isn't a consulting firm we bring in to give us expert advice on how to run our lives. The gospel life isn't something we learn *about* and then put together with instructions from the manufacturer. It's something we *become* as God does his work of creation and salvation in us and as we accustom ourselves to a life of belief and obedience and prayer.

LEAP OVER A WALL

PROVOCATION FOR PRAYER

Real help comes from GOD.
Your blessing clothes your people!

PSALM 3:8, THE MESSAGE

The language of prayer occurs primarily at one level, the personal, and for one purpose, salvation. The human condition teeters on the edge of disaster. Human beings are in trouble most of the time. Those who don't know they are in trouble are in the most trouble. Prayer is the language of the people who are in trouble and know it, and who believe or hope that God can get them out. As prayer is practiced, it moves into other level and develops other forms, but trouble—being in the wrong, being in danger, realizing that the foes are too many for us to handle—is the basic provocation for prayer.

ANSWERING GOD

HEARING AND DOING

Be doers of the word, and not
merely hearers who deceive themselves.

JAMES 1:22, NRSV

The Pharisees had an extensive and meticulous knowledge of Scripture. They revered it. They memorized it. They used it to regulate every detail of life. So why did Jesus excoriate them? Because the words were studied and not heard. For them, the Scriptures had become a book to use, not a means by which to listen to God. They isolated the book from the divine act of speaking covenantal commands and gospel promises. They separated the book from the human act of hearing that would become believing, following, and loving. Printer's ink became embalming fluid.

REVERSED THUNDER

GOD STICKS WITH US

Thank the Lord of all lords. His love never quits.

PSALM 136:3, THE MESSAGE

The central reality for Christians is the personal, unalterable, persevering commitment God makes to us. Perseverance is not the results of *our* determination, it is the result of God's faithfulness. We survive in the way of faith not because we have extraordinary stamina but because God is righteous, because God sticks with us.

A LONG OBEDIENCE

CONVERSING WITH GOD

Silence is praise to you, Zion-dwelling God,
and also obedience. You hear the prayer in it all.

PSALM 65:1, THE MESSAGE

Nearly everyone believes in God and throws casual offhand remarks in his general direction from time to time. But prayer is something quite different.

The person with whom we set aside time for intimacy, for this deepest and most personal conversation, is God. At such times the world is not banished, but it is . . . on the periphery. . . . Prayer is the desire to listen to God firsthand, to speak to God firsthand, and then setting aside the time and making the arrangements to do it. It issues from the conviction that the living God is immensely important to me.

RUN WITH THE HORSES

FAITH IS NOT FORMAL

Praise from all who love GOD!
Israel's children, intimate friends of GOD.

PSALM 148:14, THE MESSAGE

We can address God as freely as we address our parents. It is the kind of freedom that combines intimacy with reverence. We are still aware of the majesty and awesome glory of God. We do not try to reduce God to a level of coziness where we can manipulate him. The intimacy is a freedom to share *ourselves*, to express ourselves fearlessly in God's presence. We are free to be spontaneous, personal, and uninhibited. Faith is not a formal relationship hedged in with elaborate courtesies; it is a family relationship, intimate and free.

TRAVELING LIGHT

FREEDOM TO CHANGE

Tremble, Earth! You're in the Lord's presence!
In the presence of Jacob's God.

PSALM 114:7, THE MESSAGE

We do not live in an ironclad universe of cause and effect. In the presence of the God of Jacob there is life that is beyond prediction. There is freedom to change. . . .

Miracles are not interruptions of laws, which must then either be denied by worried intellectuals or defended by anxious apologists. They are expressions of freedom enjoyed by the children of a wise and exuberant Father.

WHERE YOUR TREASURE IS

A LARGER REALITY

Go out into the world uncorrupted, a breath of fresh air in this squalid and polluted society. Provide people with a glimpse . . . of the living God.

PHILIPPIANS 2:15, THE MESSAGE

Reaching out is an act of wholeness, not only for others but for us. . . . For we cannot be whole enclosed in our own habits, even if they are pious habits.

We cannot grow an oak tree in a barrel; it needs acres of earth under it and oceans of sky above it. Neither can we grow a human being in a narrow sect, a ghettoized religion. The larger the world we live in, the larger our lives develop in response. We cannot be whole human beings if we cut ourselves off from the environment that God created and in which he is working. People of faith live in a far larger reality than people without faith. "God so loved the *world*."

RUN WITH THE HORSES

GOD GIVES, WE GIVE

Don't run roughshod over the concerns
of your brothers and sisters.
Their concerns are God's concerns.

1 THESSALONIANS 4:6, THE MESSAGE

There is no history of the soul that is a single unbroken line of ascent to perfection. Peter, the apostolic rock, confessed Christ, but he also denied him. David, the man with a heart after God, sang great praises to his God, but he also grievously disobeyed him. And no history of the soul is a determined descent to damnation. . . . The prodigal was not excommunicated from the family for squandering his life. He was welcomed and enjoyed.

Life in Christ sets us free for grace. We exist in a world of giving. God gives; we give.

TRAVELING LIGHT

IN GOD'S TIME

You, GOD, are sovereign still,
always and ever sovereign.

PSALM 102:11, THE MESSAGE

Hoping is not dreaming. It is not spinning an illusion or fantasy to protect us from our boredom or our pain. It means a confident, alert expectation that God will do what he said he will do. It is imagination put in the harness of faith. It is a willingness to let God do it his way and in his time. It is the opposite of making plans that we demand that God put into effect, telling him both how and when to do it. That is not hoping in God but bullying God.

A LONG OBEDIENCE

GOD IN PERSON

Worship GOD in adoring embrace,
celebrate in trembling awe. Kiss Messiah!

PSALM 2:11, THE MESSAGE

We require an act of imagination that enables us to see that the world of God is *large*—far larger than the worlds of kings and princes, prime ministers and presidents, far larger than the worlds reported by newspaper and television. . . . We need a way to imagine—to *see*—that the world of God's ruling word is not an afterthought to the worlds of the stock exchange, the rocket launching, and summit diplomacy, but itself contains them. . . .

Psalm 2 answers our need by presenting Messiah. Messiah is God's person in history, . . . his entry into the world where people go to school, go to work, go to war, go to Chicago. He enters—and he enters *in person*.

ANSWERING GOD

THE REAL WORLD

GOD, brilliant Lord, your name
echoes around the world.

PSALM 8:9, THE MESSAGE

When we're in full possession of our powers—our education complete, our careers in full swing, people admiring us and prodding us onward—it's hard not to imagine that we're at the beginning, center, and end of the world, or at least of that part of the world in which we're placed. At these moments we need . . . to quit whatever we're doing and sit down.

When we sit down, the dust raised by our furious activity settles. . . . We become aware of the real world. *God's* world. And what we see leaves us breathless: it's so much larger, so much more full of energy and action than our ego-fueled actions, so much . . . saner than the plans we had projected.

LEAP OVER A WALL

DEALING WITH GOD

The one who plants in response to God,
letting God's Spirit do the growth work in him,
harvests a crop of real life, eternal life.

GALATIANS 6:8, THE MESSAGE

S in is not what is wrong with our minds. It is the catastrophic disorder in which we find ourselves at odds with God. This is the human condition. The facts of this disorder are all around and within us, but we would prefer to forget them. To remember them is also to remember God, and to remember God is to have to live strenuously, vigorously, and in love.

We have moments when we desire to do this, but the moments don't last long. We would rather play golf. We would rather take another battery of tests at the hospital. We would rather take another course at the university. We keep looking for ways to improve our lives without dealing with God. But we can't do it.

ANSWERING GOD

FAITHFULNESS AND OBEDIENCE

"They are no more defined by the world than I am defined by the world. Make them holy— consecrated—with truth."

JOHN 17:16–17, THE MESSAGE

The reality of the church is not accessible to secular methods of analysis. Armchair historians survey the history of the life of God's people and generalize that certain periods were more or less favorable to the spiritual prosperity of the community. I can't see that anything in the culture makes much difference. What makes the difference is faithfulness, obedience, servant-hood, prayer.

FIVE SMOOTH STONES

GOD MAKES THE CHURCH

The church is Christ's body, in which he speaks and acts, by which he fills everything with his presence.

EPHESIANS 1:23, THE MESSAGE

A church is composed of persons who live in a particular town, eat food bought in the local markets, work at jobs provided by the economy, and speak a language in common with others in the region. But it is comprised of something quite apart from the conditions of piety, culture, and politics, namely, the person of Jesus Christ. God makes the church. The Holy Spirit breathes on the chaotic and random population, "without form and void," and makes a people of God, a church. A church only has being in relation to Christ.

REVERSED THUNDER

KING AND PRIEST

GOD gave his word and he won't take it back;
you're the permanent priest, the Melchizedek priest.

PSALM 110:4, THE MESSAGE

I n antiquity (in the person of Melchizedek), the
office of king and priest had been a single, organic
function. But the functions had gotten separated so
that instead of being complementary they were
coordinated parts of a whole. The king represented
God's power to rule, shape, and guide life. The
priest represented God's power to renew, forgive,
and invigorate life. The one, associated with the
palace, operated in the external world of politics.
The other, associated with the temple, operated in
the internal world of the spirit. . . .

Then, before the eyes of a few Palestinians, it
all came together in the life of Jesus. . . .God ruled
and saved, and the two acts were the same thing.

WHERE YOUR TREASURE IS

MEETING AT THE CENTER

GOD's in charge—always. Zion's God is God for good!

PSALM 146:10, THE MESSAGE

Worship is a meeting at the center so that our lives are centered in God and not lived eccentrically. We worship so that we live in response to and from this center, the living God. Failure to worship consigns us to a life of spasms and jerks, at the mercy of every advertisement, every seduction, every siren. Without worship we live manipulated and manipulating lives. We move in either frightened panic or deluded lethargy.

People who do not worship are swept into a vast restlessness, epidemic in the world, with no steady direction and no sustaining purpose.

REVERSED THUNDER

DECEMBER

*Joy is what
God gives, not what
we work up.*

ANGELS

He ordered his angels to guard you wherever you go.

PSALM 91:11, THE MESSAGE

Angels are presented to us in two ways in Scripture. They come in the form of ordinary persons. . . . Three men appeared to Abraham and Sarah and only afterwards did they realize that their visitors were angels (Gen. 18)

The other way in which angels are presented is in visions, and then they are presented extravagantly, immense figures filling the skies, with constellations in their hair and wielding swords the size of comets.

To the devout Christian, . . . the Spirit on occasion gives visions and dreams to fortify the faithful with the knowledge that we are surrounded and supported by heavenly hosts in our warfare. Angels are for encouragement, not for entertainment.

REVERSED THUNDER

THE ABUNDANCE OF GOD

The fruit of the Spirit is love, joy, peace. . . .

GALATIANS 5:22, RSV

We come to God . . . because none of us have it within ourselves, except momentarily, to be joyous. . . .

We try to get it through entertainment. We pay someone to make jokes, . . . sing songs, . . . but that kind of joy never penetrates our lives, never changes our basic constitution. The effects are extremely temporary. . . .

We cannot make ourselves joyful. Joy cannot be commanded, purchased, or arranged. But there is something we can do. We can decide to live in response to the abundance of God and not under the dictatorship of our own poor needs.

A LONG OBEDIENCE

BE STILL

Be still, and know that I am God.

PSALM 46:10, RSV

Be still. Quit rushing through the streets long enough to become aware that there is more to life than your little self-help enterprises. When we are noisy and when we are hurried, we are incapable of intimacy—deep, complex, personal relationships. If God is the living center of redemption, it is essential that we be in touch with and responsive to that personal will.

If God has a will for this world and we want to be in on it, we must be still long enough to find out what it is (for we certainly are not going to learn by watching the evening news).

WHERE YOUR TREASURE IS

SOURCE OF LIFE

With your very own hands you formed me;
now breathe your wisdom over me.

PSALM 119:73, THE MESSAGE

In the presence of birth, we are caught up in mystery. We respond with awe. Why? We can explain the process of birth. We know all the physiological and genetic details. But none of our explanations accounts for the awe.

In the presence of birth we are at the source of life. . . . Here is mystery, but a mystery of light not darkness, full of goodness, brimming with blessing. Every birth powerfully recalls us to this source: we have our origins in someone other than ourselves, and greater than ourselves.

WHERE YOUR TREASURE IS

LIVING WATER

He Himself is our peace.

EPHESIANS 2:14, NKJV

Shalom, "peace," is one of the richest words in the Bible. You can no more define it by looking up its meaning in the dictionary than you can define a person by his or her social security number. It gathers all aspects of wholeness that result from God's will being completed in us. It is the work of God that, when complete, releases streams of living water in us and pulsates with eternal life.

Every time Jesus healed, forgave or called someone, we have a demonstration of *shalom.*

A LONG OBEDIENCE

I SEE CHRIST

When two or three of you are together because of me, you can be sure that I'll be there.

MATTHEW 18:20, THE MESSAGE

E very time I move to a new community, I find a church close by and join it. . . . I've never been anything other than disappointed. Every one turns out to be biblical, through and through: murmurers, complainers, the faithless, the inconstant, those plagued with doubt and riddled with sin, boring moralizers, glamorous secularizers.

Yet every once in a while a shaft of blazing beauty seems to break out of nowhere and illuminate these companies, and then I see what my sin-dulled eyes had missed: . . . lives of sacrificial humility, incredible courage, heroic virtue, holy praise, joyful suffering, constant prayer, persevering obedience. I see Christ.

LEAP OVER A WALL

THE EDGE OF EXPECTATION

*Embracing what God does for you is
the best thing you can do for him.*

ROMANS 12:1, THE MESSAGE

The word *Christian* means different things to different people. To one person it means a stiff, uptight, inflexible way of life, colorless and unbending. To another it means a risky, surprise-filled venture, lived tiptoe at the edge of expectation. . . .

There are numberless illustrations for either position in congregations all over the world. But if we restrict ourselves to biblical evidence, only the second image can be supported: the image of the person living zestfully, exploring every experience— pain and joy, enigma and insight, fulfillment and frustration—as a dimension of human freedom, searching through each for sense and grace.

TRAVELING LIGHT

THE WORD BECAME FLESH

The Word became flesh and blood, and
moved into the neighborhood.

JOHN 1:14, THE MESSAGE

The task of salvation is not to refine us into pure spirits so that we will not be cumbered with this too solid flesh. We are not angels, nor are we to become angels. The Word did not become a good idea, or a numinous feeling, or a moral aspiration; the Word became flesh. It also becomes flesh. Our Lord left us a command to remember and receive him in bread and wine, in acts of eating and drinking. Things matter. The physical is holy.

THE CONTEMPLATIVE PASTOR

ALL IS GIFT

Every desirable and beneficial gift
comes out of heaven.

JAMES 1:17, THE MESSAGE

Each morning we wake to a world . . . that is given by God. God *shares* who he is and what he makes, his love and his salvation. He is not just maker of heaven and earth; he is not just the revealer of truth; he is not just architect of salvation. He gives. . . .

Where all is gift, I do not own things or persons and thus don't have to protect them. Therefore I don't have to be anxious. In a world of grace I do not live in laborious struggle trying to fashion a world that suits my needs and desires, hammering together a life out of the bits and pieces of scrap lumber that come my way. I do not live in anxious suspicion, nervous about what others might do to me, what others might think of me. I simply discover and receive.

TRAVELING LIGHT

DISCIPLESHIP IS A DECISION

As the mountains are round about Jerusalem,
so the LORD is round about his people.

PSALM 125:2, RSV

My feelings are important for many things. They are essential and valuable. They keep me aware of much that is true and real. But they tell me next to nothing about God or my relation to God.

My security comes from who God is, not from how I feel. Discipleship is a decision to live by what I *know* about God, not by what I *feel* about him or myself or my neighbors. "As the mountains are round about Jerusalem, so the LORD is round about his people." The image that announces the dependable, unchanging, safe, secure existence of God's people comes from geology, not psychology.

A LONG OBEDIENCE

WISE GROWTH

Grow in grace and understanding
of our Master and Savior, Jesus Christ.

2 PETER 3:18, THE MESSAGE

When we grow, in contrast to merely change, we venture into new territory and include more people in our lives—serve more and love more. Our culture is filled with change; it's poor in growth. New things, models, developments, opportunities are announced, breathlessly, every hour. But instead of becoming ingredients in a long and wise growth, they simply replace. The previous is discarded and the immediate stuck in—until, bored by the novelty, we run after the next fad.

Men and women drawn always to the new never grow up. God's way is growth not change.

WHERE YOUR TREASURE IS

GOD IS PERSONAL

*God's eye is on those who
respect him, the ones who are looking for his love.*

PSALM 33:18, THE MESSAGE

The Hebrews were a *historical* people. They believed that God worked in their lives, *did* things. God wasn't a blurred glow of sentiment. God wasn't an abstract concept. . . . God was personal in history: creating, directing, saving, blessing. God entered the affairs of men and women, and when he did, he judged and saved, called to account and blessed. Most of all he loved.

LEAP OVER A WALL

A FRAMEWORK FOR LIFE

Lift your praising hands
to the Holy Place, and bless GOD.

PSALM 134:2, THE MESSAGE

As I entered a home to make a pastoral visit, the person I came to see was . . . embroidering a piece of cloth held taut on an oval hoop. She said, "Pastor, while waiting for you to come I realized what's wrong with me—I don't have a frame. My feelings, my thoughts, my activities—everything is loose and sloppy. There is no border to my life. . . . I need a frame for my life like this one I have for my embroidery."

How do we get that framework, . . . so that we know where we stand and are able to do our work easily and without anxiety? Christians go to worship. Week by week we enter the place of worship and get a working definition for life: the way God created us, the ways he leads us. We know where we stand.

A LONG OBEDIENCE

LOVE IS A RELATIONSHIP

If God so loved us, we also ought to love one another.

1 JOHN 4:11, RSV

The word *love*, as it is used in the biblical texts, has two obvious qualities. St. John, the master teacher on love . . . , taught that love has its origins in God ("we love, because he first loved us"—1 John 4:11) and that it is a relationship with persons ("if God so loved us, we also ought to love one another"). Love is not a word that describes my feelings. It is not a technique by which I fulfill my needs. It is not an ideal, abstract and pure, on which I meditate or discourse. It is acting in correspondence with or in response to God in relation to persons.

TRAVELING LIGHT

WALKING GOD'S WAY

Let's not allow ourselves to get fatigued
doing good. At the right time we will harvest
a good crop if we don't give up.

GALATIANS 6:9, THE MESSAGE

Christian discipleship is a decision to walk in God's ways, steadily and firmly, and then finding that the way integrates all our interests, passions, and gifts, our human needs and our eternal aspirations. It is the way of life we were created for. There are endless challenges in it to keep us on the growing edge of faith. There is always the God who sticks with us to make it possible for us to persevere.

A LONG OBEDIENCE

REAL LIFE

Let the loveliness of our Lord, our God,
rest on us, confirming the work that we do.

PSALM 90:17, THE MESSAGE

"Our citizenship is in heaven," say those who pray, and they are ardent in pursuing the prizes of that place. But this passion for the unseen in no way detracts from their involvement in daily affairs: working well and playing fair, signing petitions and paying taxes, rebuking the wicked and encouraging the righteous, getting wet in the rain and smelling the flowers. Theirs is a tremendous, kaleidoscopic assemblage of bits and pieces of touched, smelled, seen, and tasted reality that is received and offered in acts of prayer.

WHERE YOUR TREASURE IS

FREE TO GIVE

Do me a favor: Agree with each other,
love each other, be deep-spirited friends.

PHILIPPIANS 2:2, THE MESSAGE

As we acquire good things in our lives we do not become more and more independent. We do not build larger storehouses in order to preserve our riches. We find new outlets for sharing, for helping, for giving.

Even in our inadequacy, even in our weakness, even in our helplessness we are free to give. But we are not free *not* to give. Not giving is imprisoning. Not giving reduces the scope of living. Not giving—the narcissistic obsession with self—forges manacles on the spirit.

TRAVELING LIGHT

FAMILY OF FAITH

*Get along among yourselves,
each of you doing your part.*

1 THESSALONIANS 5:13, THE MESSAGE

When we become Christians, we are among brothers and sisters in faith. No Christian is an only child.

But of course, the fact that we are a family of faith does not mean we are one big happy family. The people we encounter as brothers and sisters in faith are not always nice people. They do not stop being sinners the moment they begin believing in Christ. . . . Some of them are cranky, some of them dull. . . . But at the same time our Lord tells us that they are brothers and sisters in faith. If God is my Father, then this is my family.

A LONG OBEDIENCE

WORSHIP DAZZLES US

He who sat there appeared
like jasper and carnelian, and round the throne
was a rainbow that looked like an emerald.

REVELATION 4:3, RSV

Light with the colors of precious stones (jasper, carnelian, emerald) bathes everyone gathered in worship. Lives that have been defaced by sin into blurred charcoal outlines are now seen in their true colors. Every faded tint and wavering line are restored to original sharpness and hue. Precious stones are precious because they collect and intensify light. Light is full of color, all colors, but our dull eyes are unperceptive.

"God is light and in him is no darkness at all." Worship is precious stones that reveal all the colors of light in and around us and dazzle us.

REVERSED THUNDER

KING OF KINGS

He is dressed in a robe soaked with blood, and he is addressed as "Word of God." . . . On his robe and thigh is written, KING OF KINGS, LORD OF LORDS.

REVELATION 19:13, 16, THE MESSAGE

God has made it clear that he is not content to rescue a few souls from damnation. Redemption has been conceived on a scale far exceeding our capacity to comprehend it—a new heaven and a new earth are involved.

People who pray find themselves involved both with the King who is establishing his rule in the cosmos and the Priest who is setting persons right, before God. In prayer we participate from the center to the periphery of God's oscillating personal action.

WHERE YOUR TREASURE IS

HARVEST OF HOLINESS

Oh! Teach us to live well!
Teach us to live wisely and well!

PSALM 90:12, THE MESSAGE

Holy Living is the action by which we express
in our behavior and speech the love and
presence of our Christ. Holy living is posited on
the conviction that everything we do, no matter
what we do, however common and little noticed
our lives, is connected with the action of God and
is seed that becomes either a harvest of holiness or
a vintage of wrath.

REVERSED THUNDER

PRAYER IS LANGUAGE

The first thing I want you to do is pray.
Pray every way you know how, for everyone you know.

1 TIMOTHY 2:1, THE MESSAGE

Prayer is language used in personal relation to God. It gives utterance to what we sense or want or respond to before God. God speaks to us; our answers are our prayers. The answers are not always articulate: silence, sighs, groaning—these also constitute responses. The answers are not always positive: anger, skepticism, curses—these also are responses. But always God is involved, whether in darkness or light, whether in faith or despair. This is hard to get used to. Our habit is to talk about God not to him.

ANSWERING GOD

A GOD-CENTERED WORLD

Let petitions and praises shape your worries
into prayers, letting God know your concerns.

PHILIPPIANS 4:6, THE MESSAGE

We wake each day to a world noisy with braggadocio, violent with guns, arrogant with money. What use is prayer in the face of governments, armies, and millionaires? What motivation can we muster to pray when all the obvious power is already allocated to heads of state and barons of industry?

In prayer we intend to leave the world of anxieties and enter a world of wonder. We decide to leave an ego-centered world and enter a God-centered world. We will to leave a world of problems and enter a world of mystery. But it is not easy. We are used to anxieties, egos, and problems. We are not used to wonder, God, and mystery.

ANSWERING GOD

GOD IS GREATER

*He who is in you is greater than
he who is in the world.*

1 JOHN 4:4, RSV

Nowhere in the Bible is there any attempt to answer the question, "Why does a good God permit evil?" Evil is a fact. The Bible spends a good deal of space insisting that certain facts are evil, and not minor blemishes on the surface of existence. But the Bible does not provide an explanation of evil—rather, it defines a context: all evil takes place in an historical arena bounded by Christ and prayer. Evil is not explained but surrounded. The [word of God] summarizes the context: admit evil and do not fear it—for "he who is in you is greater than he who is in the world."

REVERSED THUNDER

THE SERVANT

Here is my servant, whom I uphold,
my chosen, in whom my soul delights.

ISAIAH 42:1, NRSV

The servant role was completed in Jesus. Though there were auspicious signs that preceded and accompanied his birth, preparing the world for the majestic and kingly, the birth of Jesus itself was of the humblest peasant parentage, in an unimportant town, and in the roughest of buildings. He made a career of rejecting marks of status or privilege: he touched lepers, washed the feet of his disciples, befriended little children, encouraged women to join his entourage, and, finally, submitted to crucifixion by a foreign power. Everything about Jesus spoke of servitude.

FIVE SMOOTH STONES

FOCUS UPON GOD

Open your ears, God, to my prayer;
. . . come close and whisper your answer.

PSALM 55:1, THE MESSAGE

All of us are subject to jarring inconsistencies and dislocating contradictions. We are disoriented and stagger dizzily under the impact of accidents and disappointments. If that is all we are conscious of we go crazy and live in bedlam. We maintain sanity by living in response to that which keeps us alive: food and trust, love and shelter, clothing and forgiveness, work and leisure. The exteriors and interiors of life cohere. The clamoring needs within and the imposed necessities without find their place in a hierarchy of providence.

Prayer discovers the coordination of all needs under the mastery of the One who supplies all needs. Prayer is a focus upon God whereby all things come into focus.

REVERSED THUNDER

"LET US PRAY"

I will tell of thy name to my brethren;
in the midst of the congregation I will praise thee.

PSALM 22:22, RSV

We learn to pray by being led in prayer. We commonly think of prayer as what we do out of our own needs and on our own initiative. We experience a deep longing for God, and so we pray. We feel an artesian gush of gratitude to God, and so we pray. We are crushed with a truckload of guilt before God, and so we pray. But in a liturgy we do not take the initiative. It is not our experience that precipitates prayer. Someone stands in front of us and says, "Let us pray." We don't start it; someone else starts it, and we fall into step behind or alongside. Our egos are no longer front and center.

ANSWERING GOD

WE WORSHIP GOD

No one's ever seen or heard . . .
never so much as imagined . . . what God has
arranged for those who love him.

1 CORINTHIANS 2:9, THE MESSAGE

We worship a God who does things for us that we cannot do for ourselves. . . .

Miracles are evidence that there are dimensions to God that with all our knowledge we have not been able to anticipate. To believe in a miracle is only a way of saying that God is free— free to do a new thing. He is not bound to a deterministic creation of natural cause and effect. He is not trapped in his own cosmic machine. He is free above and beyond what we observe of his ways. He is free to do whatever he wills, whether it conforms to what we have observed as the laws he established in creation or not.

FIVE SMOOTH STONES

MATERIAL FOR GOD

The people who walked in darkness
have seen a great light.

ISAIAH 9:2, THE MESSAGE

Take a long look at the sheer quantity of wreckage around us—wrecked bodies, wrecked marriages, wrecked careers, wrecked plans, wrecked families. . . .

[Yet] we believe that the Holy Spirit is among us and within us. We believe that God's Spirit continues to hover over the chaos of the world's evil and our sin, shaping a new creation and new creatures. We believe that God is not a spectator, in turn amused and alarmed at the wreckage of world history, but a participant. . . .

We believe that everything, especially everything that looks like wreckage, is material God is using to make a praising life.

THE CONTEMPLATIVE PASTOR

SILENCE AND SOLITUDE

GOD's there, listening for all who pray,
for all who pray and mean it.

PSALM 145:18, THE MESSAGE

Prayer takes place in every detail of life, in the loneliest reaches of our hearts and the most isolated of exiles, whether geographical or emotional. There is much silence to be cultivated, and great stretches of solitude to be guarded, for these, silence and solitude, are as essential to the soul as meat and potatoes are to the body.

ANSWERING GOD

THE DIVINE REALITY

Blessed be GOD, *Israel's God!*
Bless now, bless always!

PSALM 106:48, THE MESSAGE

The Hebrews were not so much interested in understanding the human condition as they were in responding to the divine reality. . . .

Their purpose was not to understand what was going on in the human race but to be a part of what was going on with God. The Greeks were experts on understanding existence from a human point of view. The Hebrews were experts in setting human existence in response to God. Whereas the Greeks had a story for every occasion, the Hebrews had a prayer for every occasion.

WORKING THE ANGLES

ACKNOWLEDGMENTS

Grateful acknowledgment is made to the following for permission to reprint material from the published works of Eugene H. Peterson:

Answering God: The Psalms as Tools for Prayer. Copyright © 1989 by Eugene H. Peterson. Used by permission of HarperCollins Publishers, New York, NY 10022.

"Bathsheba-Gate!" *Christianity Today,* June 15, 1998. Copyright Eugene H. Peterson. Used by permission of *Christianity Today.*

The Contemplative Pastor: Returning to the Art of Spiritual Direction. Copyright © 1993 by Eugene H. Peterson. Used by permission of Wm. D. Eerdmans Publishing Co.

Five Smooth Stones. Copyright ©1980 by Eugene H. Peterson. Used by permission of Wm. D. Eerdmans Publishing Co.

Leap Over a Wall: Earthy Spirituality for Everyday Christians. Copyright © 1997 by Eugene H. Peterson. Used by permission of HarperCollins Publishers, New York, NY 10022.

Like Dew Your Youth: Growing Up With Your Teenager. Copyright © 1976, 1987, 1994 by Eugene H. Peterson. Used by permission of Wm. D. Eerdmans Publishing Co.

A Long Obedience. Copyright ©1980 InterVarsity Christian Fellowship of the USA. Used by permission of InterVarsity Press, PO Box 1400 Downers Grove, IL 60515.

"Practicing and Malpracticing the Presence of God," *Leadership Journal,* fall quarter, 1984. Copyright Eugene H. Peterson. Used by permission of *Christianity Today.*

Reversed Thunder: The Revelation of John & The Praying Imagination. Copyright © 1988 by Eugene H. Peterson. Used by permission of HarperCollins Publishers, New York, NY 10022.

Run with the Horses. Copyright © 1983 InterVarsity Christian Fellowship of the USA. Used by permission of InterVarsity Press, PO Box 1400 Downers Grove, IL 60515.

Traveling Light. Copyright © by Eugene H. Peterson. Used by permission of Helmers & Howard, Colorado Springs, CO.

Under the Unpredictable Plant: An Exploration in Vocational Holiness. Copyright © 1992 by Eugene H. Peterson. Used by permission of Wm. D. Eerdmans Publishing Co.

Where Your Treasure Is: Psalms that Summon You from Self to Community. Copyright © 1985 by Eugene H. Peterson. Used by permission of Wm. D. Eerdmans Publishing Co.

Working the Angles: The Shape of Pastoral Integrity. Copyright © 1987 by Eugene H. Peterson. Used by permission of Wm. D. Eerdmans Publishing Co.

NOTES

NOTES

NOTES

NOTES